Participatory Communication

D0613380

A Practical Guide

Thomas Tufte
Paolo Mefalopulos

THE WORLD BANK
Washington, D.C.

Copyright © 2009
The International Bank for Reconstruction and Development / The World Bank
1818 H Street, N.W.
Washington, D.C. 20433, U.S.A.
All rights reserved
Manufactured in the United States of America
First Printing: June 2009

  Printed on recycled paper

1 2 3 4 5   12 11 10 09

ISBN-13: 978-0-8213-8008-6
eISBN: 978-0-8213-8010-9
ISSN: 1726-5878   DOI: 10.1596/978-0-8213-8008-6

Cover photo by Curt Carnemark

Library of Congress Cataloging-in-Publication Data has been requested.

Contents

Tables

Figures

Boxes

Preface

What do we mean when we say participatory communication? What are the practical implications of working with participatory communication strategies in development and social change processes? What experiences exists in practice that documents that participatory communication adds value to a development project or program?

The aim of this user guide on participatory communication is to provide answers to some of these questions. Many communication practitioners and development workers face obstacles and challenges in their practical work. A participatory communication strategy offers a very specific perspective on how to articulate social processes, decision-making processes, and any change process for that matter. Participatory approaches are nothing new. However, what is new is the proliferation of institutions, especially governmental but also nongovernmental organizations (NGOs), that seek participatory approaches in their development initiative.

This guide seeks to provide perspectives, tools and experiences regarding how to go about it with participatory communication strategies. It is conceived as a guide to be of relevance and utility for development workers in the field. It is targeted at both at government and their officials, World Bank staff, and at civil society.

The particular relevance of this guide is three-fold:

- placing the practitioner debate about participatory communication within a **conceptual framework,** allowing the practitioner who reads this to position him- or herself conceptually, understanding some of the possible implications of opting for one or another strategic approach in their use of communication
- **providing an introduction** to the use of a participatory communication approach to specific development projects as well as illustrating the use of participatory communication in broader social change processes.
- **drawing generic lessons learned** from the experiences with participatory communication

It is thus our hope that this user guide in participatory communication will contribute to the formulation of communication strategies that again can enhance dynamic, engaging, and sustainable change processes.

Finally, we would like to thank those people who participated in the review of the draft document. We thank Line Friberg, Karen Reiff, Obadiah Tohomdet, Tony Lambino, and Barbara Catherwood. A special thanks goes to Florencia Enghel who challenged us by raising many questions as well as providing us with very detailed comments. Finally, we should acknowledge the contribution of the Danish Ministry of Foreign Affairs that made this publication possible.

Thomas Tufte and Paolo Mefalopulos
Copenhagen and Washington, DC.
January 20, 2009

CHAPTER 1

Development Communication

Trends in Development Communication

The discipline of development communication, both as theory and as practice, emerged closely interconnected with the growing "development industry." From the outset "development support communication," "program support communication," "communication for development," or as called in this publication, "development communication," has been seen as a strategic tool to persuade people to change and enhance development processes.

Many communication models have informed the field. The early models like Lasswell's communication theory (1948) were linear in their understanding of communication, which was understood as a transfer of information, leading to foreseeable step-by-step change processes, as it is shown in its model illustrated below. These processes were usually identified with changes in behaviors much in line with the development thinking of the modernization paradigm. Persuasion theory, originating from the advertising industry, also became a strategy to achieve information transfer.

Throughout the 1970s and 1980s, strategic communication approaches to enhance individual behavior change evolved to be known as behavior change communication (BCC). Behavior change communication is associated closely with social marketing. Social marketing strategies are a means to promote particular behaviors or social norms via communication interventions. Social marketing is widely used in health communication, including family planning, and more recently in HIV/AIDS communication.

In these early models of strategic communication, there were no participatory elements. The assumption was that the power of communication to enhance development was in the correct crafting of the content and in the adequate targeting of audiences. The goal was individual behavior change.

Table 1.1. Lasswell's Theory

Who?	Says what?	In what channel?	To whom?	With what effect?
Refers to the senders/ those taking decisions about communication goals and approaches?	Refers to the content and how to package it (i.e. the message)	Decides which media should be used	Refers to the audiences of the communication initiative	Evaluates the impact of communication

By the early 1990s, budget line items for Information, Education and Communication (IEC) activities began to be incorporated more systematically within development projects. Typically these activities are nonparticipatory in approach, emphasizing dissemination of information via the production of audio-visual or print materials.

Two models of communication came to dominate. First, the diffusion model of communication emerged, which relies heavily on the practice and theory of Everett Rogers (1962), emerged. Second, during the 1950s, experiences with participatory communication first appeared when Brazilian adult educator Paulo Freire worked with adult literacy campaigns among the poor peasants in North-eastern Brazil.[1] Freire's original literacy work empowered landless peasants to formulate their own demands for a better life and to liberate themselves from oppressive conditions. From this experience, he grew into one of the most influential proponents for participatory communication theory and practice. Central to this line of thinking was the emphasis on letting the stakeholders get involved in the development process and determine the outcome, rather than imposing a pre-established (i.e. already decided by external actors) outcome.

From the outset the focus of participatory communication was on dialogical communication rather than on linear communication. The emphasis was on participatory and collective processes in research, problem identification, decision-making, implementation, and evaluation of change.

Most recently participatory approaches to communication have reinforced the emphasis on structural and social change. A broad-based policy debate initiated by the Rockefeller Foundation in 1997 and pursued by the Communication for Social Change Consortium in subsequent years has focused on structural inequality and social transformation. The "Rockefeller process" led to a definition of communication for social change as "a process of public and private dialogue through which people themselves define who they are, what they need and how to get what they need in order to improve their own lives. It utilizes dialogue that leads to collective problem identification, decision making, and community-based implementation of solutions to development issues" (www.communicationforsocialchange.org).

Another line of thinking within development communication focuses on life skills development. This deals with the issues of developing core competencies required to engage actively as a citizen in society. This approach developed through the 1990s with a close connection to formal and informal education. Areas such as health education, civic education, income generation, and human rights are the core competencies associated with life skills development, and the forms of communication are didactic and face-to-face. Life skills development initiatives are performed in both formal and informal educational contexts.

This booklet uncovers the principles and practices of participatory communication to guide communication practitioners through the different ways to work with participation in solving current development problems.

A Call for Participation

While the quest for participation in development programs and projects has existed for a long time, in recent years it has gained voice and become a stronger concern. Participation is a principle in development with support coming from many different stakeholders: governments, donors, civil society, and ordinary citizens

From the 1970s and onwards, voices of both development practitioners and academics from developing countries have raised fundamental questions about the Western domination of the work and debate in development. The questions include who voices the concerns of the poorest and most marginalized populations, how is policy developed, and who participates in the decision-making processes? At the core of these concerns lies the quest for participation of the "voiceless" from developing countries—the marginalized and poorest sectors, as well as the disabled and women—in the international policy development and debate, as well as in the practical day-to-day work of implementing development projects. These questions have gained resonance today among many of the larger institutions working with development.

An early critique comes from Latin America through Freire's work in Brazilian adult education. He produced seminal works on the history of participatory communication, particularly his books on liberating pedagogy (1979) and his critique of extension work (1973). The section on defining participation contains an elaboration of his dialogical communication model, which emphasizes a close dialectic between collective action and reflection and works towards empowerment.

Additional early Latin American contributions to participatory strategies included scholars and practitioners who, in line with the dependency paradigm's national discourse, were critical of the international (Western) centers. They were also inspired by the resistance movements against military dictatorships and the pro-democracy movement across Latin America, especially in the 1980s. Examples of this critical thinking and concern about people's participation are reflected in the academic works of British development researcher Robert Chambers (1983) and Colombian development researcher Arturo Escobar (1995).

Within development practice in the course of the 1990s and into the new millennium, these critical approaches to the dominant development discourses grew. From the large UN summits through the 1990s to the world social forums in recent years, with a growing voice civil society has articulated questions and concerns about participation in the development discourse, policy process, and actual practice. Transnational advocacy networks within a growing global civil society have provided innovative spaces for the participation paradigm to evolve into an ever more resonant quest for the contributions of the voiceless, the poorest, and marginalized sectors. As promises of past paradigms fail to materialize, the demand for a shift from expert-driven models to endogenous ones grows steadily.

The international development community has been attentive to the issues raised. Today participation, along with concerns for voice, empowerment, and poverty orientation, is at the core of much development work, particularly in governance issues. Participatory approaches are present in project cycles of many organizations.

Keywords: Critique of development discourses, endogenous models, focus on participation

Defining Participation

Stakeholders often have very different visions and definitions of participation in development. Therefore, for development practitioners to be clear on their conceptual approach to participation, a series of important questions have to be answered:

- What is participation to each stakeholder?
- Why is participation so important in development processes, and for whom is it important?
- Who is supposed to participate?
- When is participation relevant, and for whom?
- What are the most common constraints to participation, and according to whom?
- How is a successful participatory process evaluated?

No consensus exists around a common definition of participation: it varies depending on the perspective applied. Some stakeholders define participation as the mobilization of people to eliminate unjust hierarchies of knowledge, power, and economic distribution. Others define it as the reach and inclusion of inputs by relevant groups in the design and implementation of a development project. These examples represent two of the main approaches to participation: *a social movement perspective* and *a project-based or institutional perspective*. These perspectives share a common understanding of participation as the involvement of ordinary people in a development process leading to change. Their scope and methods, however, can differ.

Why is a participatory approach required? There are several answers. From the institutional perspective mentioned above, participation can be used a tool to achieve a pre-established goal defined by someone external to the community involved. For the social movement mentioned above, participation itself can be a goal as an empowering process. There is, however, growing consensus for active participation in the early stages of a development project or program, both in research and design of interventions. Such participatory goal setting does not secure a continued role for participation in the following stages of project implementation. It only indicates that with ownership in setting goals a sustained process with relevant outcomes and impact will be possible.

Furthermore, the fundamental aim of empowering people to handle challenges and influence the direction of their own lives is inherent in participation. In Deepa Narayan's definition of empowerment, participation becomes a turning point: "Empowerment is the expansion of assets and capabilities of poor people to participate in, negotiate with, influence, control, and hold accountable institutions that affect their lives" (Narayan 2006: 5). Narayan's perspective is the institutional one, where participation for empowerment is about strengthening the people's capacities and the demand side of governance.

In summary, a continuum of outcomes, beyond the more tangible outputs, can be identified when participatory strategies are applied in an intervention. These outcomes can include the following:

- Psycho-social outcomes of increased *feelings of ownership* of a problem and a commitment to do something about it
- *Improvement of competencies and capacities* required to engage with the defined development problem
- Actual *influence on institutions* that can affect an individual or community

These illustrate that participation produces outcomes at least three levels:

- Individual psycho-social level
- Life skills level, emphasizing the acquirement of competencies
- Institutional level or the level of community development

Keywords: Goal versus tool, participatory strategies result in a continuum of outcomes: ownership, commitment, competencies, capacities, institutional influence.

Participation as a Method in Development Projects

This section explores how participation can be used by development organizations, ranging from international agencies to civil society organizations. Within this landscape of organizations, participation is an essential tool in development projects:

- **Providing basic services effectively** – Mechanisms of public or private service provision, including health, education, transport, agricultural extension and water, entail strategies that are affordable and inclusive even of marginalized groups.
- **Pursuing advocacy goals** – Collection of data from ordinary citizens feeds their voice into policy formulation processes. A key element to achieve this input is support of civil society and local governance initiatives, such as popular participation in public budgeting and individual and community empowerment programs that strengthen the voice of marginalized groups. Furthermore, advocacy has grown significantly in recent years as an NGO activity.
- **Monitoring progress towards goals** – These activities include self-reporting schemes and direct community involvement in monitoring processes.
- **Facilitating reflection and learning among local groups** – Opportunities for dialogue, learning and critique become central elements in evaluating a project or program.

Stages of a Participatory Development Project

Each project issue can be divided into stages, and this division facilitates assessment of when and to what degree a participatory approach is relevant. From an institutional perspective, there are four key stages of a development project:

1. **Research Stage** is where the development problem is accurately defined. All relevant stakeholders can be involved in this process. The research around the development problem can include studying previous experiences, individual

and community knowledge and attitudes, existing policies and other relevant contextual information related to socio-economic conditions, culture, spirituality, gender, etc.

2. **Design Stage** defines the actual activities. A participatory approach helps to secure the ownership and commitment of the communities involved. Active participation by local citizens and other stakeholders aims to enhance both the quality and relevance of the suggested interventions.

3. **Implementation Stage** is when the planned intervention is implemented. Participation at this stage increases commitment, relevance and sustainability.

4. **Evaluation Stage** participation ensures that the most significant changes are voiced, brought to common attention and assessed. For a meaningful evaluation, indicators and measurements should be defined in a participatory process at the very beginning of the initiative involving all relevant stakeholders.

Chapter 3 provides an in-depth look at how to make a participatory approach to communication operational at every stage. If all activities incorporate authentic, or highest-level, participation, empowerment results.

> **Keywords**: Participation as tool: allows service provision; enables voice; allows monitoring via self-reporting; facilitates critical reflection and learning. Participation in four stages of a project: research, design, implementation and evaluation.

A Typology of Participation

Cutting across the distinctions of participation as a goal versus participation as a tool used in specific project stages allows different perceptions of participation to be identified. Each of the categories below refers to different levels of participation and communication (see also Mefalopulos 2008: 91ff). When initiating a development project or program, it is useful to clarify what perception of participation will guide the strategy conceptually. Stretching the concept, four perceptions can be identified:

- **Passive participation** is the least participatory of the four approaches. Primary stakeholders of a project participate by being informed about what is going to happen or has already happened. People's feedback is minimal or non-existent, and their participation is assessed through methods like head counting and contribution to the discussion (sometimes referred to as participation by information).

- **Participation by consultation** is an extractive process, whereby stakeholders provide answers to questions posed by outside researchers or experts. Input is not limited to meetings but can be provided at different points in time. In the final analysis, however, this consultative process keeps all the decision-making power in the hands of external professionals who are under no obligation to incorporate stakeholders' input.

- **Participation by collaboration** forms groups of primary stakeholders to participate in the discussion and analysis of predetermined objectives set by the project. This level of participation does not usually result in dramatic changes in what should be accomplished, which is often already determined. It does, however, require an active involvement in the decision-making process about how to achieve it. This incorporates a component of horizontal communication and capacity building among all stakeholders—a joint collaborative effort. Even if initially dependent on outside facilitators and experts, with time collaborative participation has the potential to evolve into an independent form of participation.

■ **Empowerment participation** is where primary stakeholders are capable and willing to initiate the process and take part in the analysis. This leads to joint decision making about what should be achieved and how. While outsiders are equal partners in the development effort, the primary stakeholders are *primus inter pares*, i.e., they are equal partners with a significant say in decisions concerning their lives. Dialogue identifies and analyzes critical issues, and an exchange of knowledge and experiences leads to solutions. Ownership and control of the process rest in the hands of the primary stakeholders.

Keywords: Passive participation, consultation, functional participation, empowerment participation

Conceptual Challenges in a Participatory Communication Model

When approaching a development problem from a communications perspective, to what conceptual approaches should one refer?

In the multiplicity of communication approaches applied in development over the years, two main schools dominate and co-exist in today's development practice. On one hand, the diffusion model encompasses a broad range of strategies aiming to solve problems due to "lack of knowledge and information." External change agents drive the processes, with little to no room for participation. This approach is linear, monologue-like, top-down communication.

On the other hand, is the participatory model based on Freire's liberating pedagogy from the 1960s, renewed in more recent debates about development? This school takes globalization, transnational networking, new media and governance into account. These issues help to determine the strategic communication objectives. Rather than communicating the correct or relevant information to specific audiences, it is about articulating processes of collective action and reflection by relevant stakeholders. The center of attention is the empowerment of citizens by their active involvement in the identification of problems, development of solutions and implementation of strategies. The participatory model is a dialogic and horizontal approach to communication and development.

The Life Skills Training Model can be considered as the intermediary model of development communication (Hendricks 1998). In life skills training, the focus is on the development of personal skills. This approach also originates in adult education, but in development work it is connected with rights-based approaches, as well as with addressing structural conditions that impede skills development.

We can summarize the conceptual approaches to development communication in the heuristic framework shown in table 1.2.

Table 1.2. The Conceptual Approaches to Development Communication

Development Communication	The Diffusion Model (one-way/monologic communication)	The Life Skills Model	The Participatory Model (two-way/dialogic communication)
Definition of the problem	Lack of information	Lack of information and skills	Lack of stakeholders' engagement
Notion of culture	Culture as obstacle	Culture as ally	Culture as "way of life"
Notion of catalyst	External change agent	External catalyst in partnership with the community	Joint partnership (external and internal)
Notion of education	Banking pedagogy	Life skills, didactics	Liberating pedagogy
Notion of groups of references	Passive: targets audiences	Active: targets trainee groups	Active: targets citizen/stakeholders
How you are communicating	Messages to persuade	Messages and experiences	Social issues engaged, problem-posing, dialogue
Main notion of change	Individual behavior	Individual behavior, social norms, experiential learning	Individual and social behavior, social norms, power relations
Expected outcome	Change of individual behavior, numerical results	Change of individual behavior, increased skills	Articulation of political and social processes, sustainable change, collective action
Duration of activity	Short- and mid-term	Short- and mid-term	Mid- and long-term

The nine parameters in the left column are a conceptual checklist to work within the earliest stages of developing a participatory communication strategy. Thus, a conceptual clarity can emerge from discussing these parameters. This discussion can relate the parameters to the four stages (research, design, implementation, evaluation) of a participatory development project, as well as to the typology of participation (passive, consultation, collaboration, empowerment) both presented earlier in this chapter. A closer analysis of participatory communication follows in Chapter 2.

Notes

[1] Participatory approaches have been also adopted in other sectors, such as forestry, where the shift from RRA (Rapid Rural Appraisal) to PRA (Participatory Rural Appraisal) is considered one of the most significant.

Participatory Communication

History and Vision: A Snapshot

The vision of using new technologies to pursue better lives for humankind has always existed, and it was reinforced throughout the 20th century with each new technological advancement. In 1927 the German author Bertolt Brecht formulated a "radio theory" in which he envisioned the new technology, the radio, as a *dialogical instrument for change*: "Change this apparatus over from distribution to communication... On this principle the radio should step out of the supply business and organize its listeners as suppliers" (Brecht 1927). It was in many ways a precursor to the theory and practice of participatory communication, as well as of interactive media such as the internet.

In the years that followed Brecht's early vision, the radio lost its dialogic potential as it developed into a mass mediated broadcasting instrument. However, today's rapid spread of community radio, as well as the growth of digital radio and interactive radio program formats, revives the participatory potential of radio technology.

Brecht's work contains the two core visions still inherent today in participatory communication: first, technologies possess the potential to improve the lives of many people by giving them a voice; second, his groundwork laid out the educational principles inherent in many of today's participatory communication models—dialogical communication.

Brecht's educational principles have inspired many in innovative theatre, including Brazilian theatre practitioner Augusto Boal. Developed in the 1970s, his ideas from Forum Theatre brought principles of participatory theatre a step further, and they are still spreading around the world (Boal 1974).

In the 1960s and 1970s, the Colombian sociologist Orlando Fals Borda developed participatory action research (PAR) as a methodology involving stakeholders in the identification of the core issues in development process. Later in the 1980s, Robert Chambers, a research associate at the Institute of Development Studies in Sussex, UK, was instrumental in developing a successful methodology for community facilitation known as Participatory Rural Appraisal (PRA). PRA makes people express their own knowledge and conduct their own analysis, assessment, and action planning.

Keywords: Providing a voice, dialogical communication.

Conceptual Framework

When applying a participatory approach to communication in development projects, there are key questions and a framework of guiding principles to lead practitioners and stakeholders. The following are key questions to consider:

- What is the development problem to address: information, lack of skills, or social inequality?
- What notion of culture is inherent in the proposed approach?
- Is the catalyst or change agent understood?
- What principles guide the understanding of education?
- Are there active stakeholders or audiences to address? What are their respective roles in the communication process?
- What messages will be communicated: examples, life experiences or social issues?
- What is the aim of the change: individual behaviors, social norms, power relations, social or economic structures?
- How will outcomes be monitored and evaluated?
- What is the time perspective to achieve the desired changes?

These questions are relevant to pose prior to any communication for development intervention. Chapter 3 will move a step further and provide practical guidelines and illustrations of how the monologic and dialogic approaches to communication for development can apply participation.

Guiding Principles

A number of principles emerge as fundamental to participatory communication. These principles stem from globally influential thinkers and contribute to the framework under which participatory communication has evolved. Although not an exhaustive list, the following are some of the most important principles:

Dialogue

The free and open dialogue remains the core principle of participatory communication. Paulo Freire defines dialogue as "the encounter between men in order to name the world. Those who have been denied their primordial right to speak their word must first reclaim this right and prevent the continuation of this act of exclusion." For Freire, the free and open dialogue whereby people can "name the world" is voice, the principle of action-reflection-action and horizontal communication.

In project language, the process of "naming the world" is called problem definition. Rather than just a lack of information, the type of problems defined in such dialogues can be of social or economic nature, issues of inequality or injustice. In defining the problem this way, the communication strategy to be developed will entail a different pathway than if it were one of information, whereby diffusion-oriented solutions would be suggested.

Voice

Central to dialogic communication is a consciousness of power relations contained in any human relationship. Freire's concern was a shift in power, giving voice to marginalized groups, time and space to articulate their concerns, to define their problems, to formulate solutions, and to act on them. The role of the media in participatory communication possesses similar concerns. Supporting and strengthening community media can ensure the most marginalized groups have a platform to voice their concerns, engage in public debate and solve problems.

Liberating Pedagogy

For dialogic communication to happen, someone or something has to articulate the process. This catalyst is typically a person,[1] either internal to the community or external, acting to facilitate the dialogue. A radio or television program could also serve as the catalyst. According to Freire, however, the objective of the catalyst is not only to offer relevant solutions to pre-defined problems, thus simply disseminating information from the informed to the uninformed in a non-participatory manner. Rather, the catalyst would articulate a dialogue whereby collective problem identification and solution would take place (Freire 1970).

For this liberating pedagogy to take place, Freire outlined four pillars on which to communicate: love, humility (the absence of arrogance), faith and hope. The logical consequence is the establishment of mutual trust. The result of a liberating pedagogy based on dialogue is what he termed *"conscientizacão,"* which translates roughly into action-oriented awareness raising. Freire's liberating pedagogy contrasts what he called a "banking pedagogy" of depositing information in the minds of people (see the conceptual framework in Chapter 1).

Action-Reflection-Action

Despite the emphasis on dialogue and reflection, participatory communication is also strongly action oriented. As a crucial ingredient of participatory communication, the empowerment process is based on reflection on problems, but also on integration of action—the attempt to act collectively on the problem identified. It grounds the "talk" in real life problems.

Key results of participatory communication are the articulation of awareness raising and commitment to action. First and foremost, it becomes a process of empowerment for involved communities that feel commitment to and ownership of the problem. Issues of leadership lay inherent in the attention given to the catalyst, and the emphasis of the collective nature of the process speaks to the need for mutually reinforcing the commitment to change, as well as speaking to the actual issue of power.

Today these guiding principles are widely recognized as the foundation of most participatory communication. In the 1970s, the Bolivian communication pioneer Luiz Ramiro Beltrán spoke of "horizontal communication" as a way of pinpointing what participatory communication brings to the table, which is significantly different from the diffusion- and effects-oriented communication models (Beltrán 1979).

Keywords: Naming the world, true dialogue, voice, power, liberating pedagogy, catalyst, *concientizacão*, action-reflection-action, horizontal communication.

Participatory Spaces: The Role of the Media

Access to spaces of communication and dialogue is crucial, as mentioned previously. This access is also a crucial step in the participatory communication assessment, which will be elaborated in Chapter 3. What is often not made explicit in participatory communication approaches, however, is the important role of media access, which is increasingly crucial considering the rapid changes in media tools, coverage and worldwide use. Thus, participatory communication is also about visibility and voice in the mediated public sphere, which leads us to ask further: what more concrete roles do the media play in participatory communication?

While some of the diffusion-oriented, monologic models of communication focus on national mass media's key roles in communication interventions, the more participatory strategies emphasize media that allows more dialogue, such as community-based media. Whether media serve only as channels of communication or whether they become catalysts of social mobilization and change in themselves is another distinction. The Colombian scholar Clemencia Rodriguez argues in her book, *Fissures in the Mediascape*, "citizen media are highly participatory by providing access and space for people to participate in all phases of media production" (Rodriguez, 2001).

Furthermore, another distinction regards choice of medium—whether to use mass media or face-to-face communication like theatre or concerts. Linked to this choice is a concern for how the chosen media and communication formats are used. For example, theatre can be used not only for one-way communication but also in very participatory and dialogical ways, as in Augusto Boal's Forum Theatre.

Over the years, a series of concepts have emerged emphasizing different aspects of media's role in participatory communication processes. F. Ogboajah spoke in the mid 1980s of the "Oramedia" in Africa. These media were all the popular forms of communication from poetry and folk tales to theatre and musical concerts. They were grounded in indigenous culture and both produced and consumed by members of a group, reinforcing the values of that group. This concept stresses not only the cultural characteristics of these media but also the people's participation in their production and consumption. With a more political approach, the concept of "Alternative Media" emerged in Latin America in the 1970s to signify the grassroots media—community radios, murals, video documentaries—in opposition to the mainstream media. These came to symbolize a resistance platform in the fight against the military dictatorships and provided a space for the voice and visibility of oppressed groups under these regimes. In 1984, British-American John Downing coined "Radical Media" and Clemencia Rodriguez the concept of "Citizen Media" in 2001. Each in their own way, these theories incorporate aspects of citizenship and people's participation.

In developing participatory communication strategies, media-specific concerns evolve around the following issues:

- Types of media: from folk, community, and mass media to the new media of internet and satellite communication
- Levels of media: local and community-based media to national and transnational media

- Nature of media: electronic media, one-way or interactive, face-to-face communication
- Institutional characteristics of media: from public to private, national to community-owned, free and independent to closely government controlled
- Economic logic informing the media: commercial media, non-profit media, and mixed models.

Does the existing media environment stimulate dialogue and empowerment processes? This question needs to be answered to assess how and to what degree collaboration with media can contribute to giving voice and visibility to the communities involved.

The list of related media issues could be expanded to include a distinction between analog versus digital media, state of legal regulation of the media, diversification of media types, massification of access. These are keywords that describe the process leading to a new media scenario where new opportunities are provided for people and groups to be directly involved in program development and management.

Keywords: Media access, community-based media, culture and Oramedia, politics and alternative media, citizenship and citizens media, new media scenario

Combining Theory with Practice: The Multi-Track Model

The multi-track model originated from the need to combine the richness and complexity of operational approaches and development challenges into a consistent methodological communication framework. To highlight its flexibility and adaptability to various situations, this model divides its approaches to communication into two basic categories: monologic communication and dialogic communication.

Monologic communication comprises one-way communication approaches such as information dissemination, media campaigns, and other diffusion approaches. Dialogic communication approaches refer to two-way communication, where the process and its outputs are open-ended and the scope explores issues and generates new knowledge and solutions, rather than just transmits information. Table 2.1 illustrates the main features of these two communication modes.

Table 2.1. The Main Features of Communication Modes

	MONOLOGIC (one-way communication)		DIALOGIC (two-way communication)	
	Communication to Inform	Communication to Persuade	Communication to Explore	Communication to Empower
Main purpose	Raise awareness, increase knowledge	Promote attitude and behavior change	Assess, probe and analyze issues, prevent conflicts	Build capacities, involve stakeholders
Main model of reference	One-way (monologic)	One-way (monologic)	Two-way (dialogic)	Two-way (dialogic)
Preferred methods and media	Predominant use of mass media	Predominant use of media	Heavy use of interpersonal method	Use of dialogue to promote participation

This categorization shows clearly what communication methods and tools should be used in specific initiatives. No approach fits universally, but each should be applied appropriately according to circumstances and desired objectives. Similar to the others, the multi-track model divides a communication program into four main phases: research, strategy design, implementation, monitoring, and evaluation. However, differently from the other models that are defined by one of the two modes, the multi-track model divides and combines the two according to the needs of each phase.

In the first phase, the dialogic mode should be the guiding principle, since in any investigation key stakeholders build trust and seek solutions jointly. In this way, dialogue and two-way communication become necessary to reconcile different perceptions and positions and to define the priorities for the development initiatives. Since the objectives of the communication initiatives are identified and decided in phase one, the initiative is shaped through a participatory approach, even if an imperfect one.

The objectives set in the first phase will decide the communication modes of reference of the other phases. If the objectives are a health campaign to prevent the spread of avian flu, for instance, the communication strategy may be based on monologic, one-way approaches. Instead, if mobilizing communities to take a more active part is the strategy, many of the communication approaches will be dialogic. Other cases may be a more balanced combination of both approaches.

Hence, the multi-track is an integrated and project-oriented model, combining different approaches within a flexible framework. It always requires dialogue with all key stakeholders during the initial stages, problem identification and research of an initiative, no matter what the purpose or the sector of the intervention. After this the approach becomes truly multi-track, using a variety of approaches appropriate to the situation. The various approaches—information dissemination, social marketing, lobbying, community mobilization and others—are considered tracks and intended as actions or paths to be followed. This model is not simply the sum of different communication approaches: it has a consistent theoretical and methodological framework, which is capable of containing the major differences of the two opposing paradigms without incurring in basic contradictions.

The participatory communication paradigm does not call for a replacement of the basic communication functions associated with information dissemination, but rather broadens its boundaries to include more interactive ways of communicating. This new conception contains functions of both communication modes: the monologic and the dialogic. When the two are fully understood and properly applied, if needed combined together, development communication is used to its fullest advantage (see examples in Chapter 3 and 4).

The theoretical conception of the multi-track model considers communication fundamentally as a horizontal and participatory process, at least in the crucial initial stages. It also acknowledges that in development there are information gaps and areas of needed change that can be supported effectively by approaches linked to the linear flow of monologic models. Such approaches, or communication tracks, however, would be used only after the horizontal communicative process occurs and determines the objectives of the intervention in a participatory way.

Whenever local stakeholders are not engaged from the beginning of the intervention, the possibilities for problems and failures rise dramatically. Examples are innumerable in which communication failed to achieve expected changes due to people's initial lack of involvement or to their limited or contradictory understanding of issues by various stakeholders. That specific behavior changes cannot be achieved without recognition of wider social acceptance and/or changes is increasingly acknowledged.

The fact that the two main communication perspectives, monologic (one-way) and dialogic (two-way), rely on different theoretical perspectives and methodological frameworks should not be considered as contradictory, but rather as an asset capable of better addressing the complexity of many situations. This asset derives its strength from the selective and purposeful use of specific communication approaches applied according to the objectives of the initiative.

When dealing with the challenges of each individual phase of a communication program (research/communication-based assessment, strategy design, implementation and evaluation), it is easier to see what type of communication to apply for which purpose. The research phase must always be based on two-way communication methods and is most effective in investigating, assessing, and uncovering key issues. This greatly reduces the possibility of relying on incorrect assumptions and avoids the risk of alienating relevant stakeholders by leaving them out of the decision-making process. After this phase, approaches of both modes can be used according to the needs and scope of the initiative.

Different from other models, the multi-track approach selects and combines different communication approaches into a unified grand approach. The differences between the two modalities, however, remain significant. The monologic/diffusion mode and its tracks can be considered as a close-ended linear communication flow. When tracks such as social marketing or Information, Education and Communication (IEC) are designed and implemented, the end objectives are always defined from the start.

The dialogic mode instead can be considered a circular, open-ended process, since the objectives are usually not specifically defined, and even when they are, they can be changed according to the output of the investigation. The primary goal of the two-way communication process is not to persuade audiences to adopt a predefined change but rather to engage stakeholders to explore the situation and define the needed change.

How each perspective defines or conceives a communication objective and the relative implications for evaluating the impact of the intervention reflects the difference between the two modes. In diffusion approaches, the communication objective requires changes in awareness, knowledge, attitude or behaviors/practices of specific groups of people. A baseline study before and after the intervention assesses the impact, while other variables that may interfere with the communication are taken into account.

Dialogic communication objectives assess risks, identify opportunities, prevent problems and identify or confirm needed change. Being the results of a heuristic process, in most cases the objectives cannot be specifically defined beforehand. The impact of such an open-ended and process-oriented approach to communication is much harder to measure accurately. How to measure trust, empowerment, better project design, consensus-seeking, and problem prevention is still an unresolved issue.

In summary, the multi-track approach combines the theoretical potential of the main development communication families with their rich range of practical applications. This model uses theoretical interpretation to guide the selection and application of specific communication approaches, according to the needs and circumstances of specific initiatives. DevComm's experiences in a number of projects confirm the value-added of this approach, however, more long-term and systematic studies are needed to accurately assess its effectiveness.

Notes

[1] This would certainly be one of the key tasks of the "new communicator" or communication specialist.

CHAPTER 3

Applying Participatory Communication in Development Projects

Participatory Communication in Action

Participation and communication are terms with broad and multifaceted connotations, trying to define them specifically is a difficult task. Even harder is providing a widely acceptable definition of participatory communication. For the scope of this book, participatory communication is an approach based on dialogue, which allows the sharing of information, perceptions and opinions among the various stakeholders and thereby facilitates their empowerment, especially for those who are most vulnerable and marginalized. Participatory communication is not just the exchange of information and experiences: it is also the exploration and generation of new knowledge aimed at addressing situations that need to be improved.

To be genuinely participatory and truly effective,[1] communication should occur among all parties affected, ensuring all have similar opportunities to influence the outcome of the initiative. Optimally participatory communication would be part of the whole project process, from beginning to end. Since this approach promotes the active involvement of stakeholders in investigating options and shaping decisions regarding development objectives, participatory communication also facilitates empowerment. In this way, the effects go beyond the project boundaries, spilling into the wider social and political dimensions.

The literature on development programs is increasingly flooded by examples of projects apparently embracing "participation." At a closer look, however, very few cases meet the standards of genuine participation. This publication, while embracing a broad range of applications, promotes the highest form of participatory communication applications, empowerment communication (defined in Chapter 1).

Proper applications of participatory communication methods and tools are not enough to ensure a project's success. Broader contextual requirements are also needed, namely a flexible project framework (especially in terms of timelines); a politically conducive environment, allowing open and transparent communication; and an enabling attitude by key stakeholders, including project management. Close adherence to these factors is essential for a high level of participation, while lack of these preconditions usually results in lower participation.

It should be highlighted that within the current structure of the development aid system it is rather difficult to have a high degree of participation. The agenda of projects and programs is often set by a few individuals (for example, policy makers or technocrats) with very little input from other stakeholders, especially at the local level. Moreover, the rigid management procedures and the tight deadlines for planning and funding required for approving and implementing projects allows little flexibility needed for participatory processes.

Finally, it should be noted how participation and participatory communication tend to be associated with grassroots and community-driven development. While this is often the case, it should be acknowledged that participatory communication could be used at any level of decision making (local, national, international) regardless of the diversity of groups involved, even if the number of people involved can significantly affect its effectiveness. There are instances where participatory communication has been used to enhance social accountability in water reforms, to engage parliamentarians in governance reforms and to mediate conflicts between local communities and national authorities.

Value-added and benefits

To reinforce the benefits of adopting participatory communication, it is important to understand that participation and participatory communication are main answers to why so many development initiatives in the 1970s and 1980s did not achieve their objectives to produce significant improvements for the many poor of the planet. The causes of many such failures were ascribed to the limited understanding of local context and the insufficient involvement of local stakeholders. In addition, misunderstandings and differences in perceptions about key problems often led to limited political buy-in and faulty project design.

By actively engaging stakeholders from the start and by seeking a broader consensus around development initiatives, participatory communication has begun to be considered a crucial tool to avoid past mistakes. Many conflicts and obstacles can be prevented if addressed in a timely fashion. Moreover, genuine participation increases the sense of project ownership by local stakeholders, thus enhancing sustainability. On one hand, communication practitioners might have a more complex process to take into account the many viewpoints to be reconciled, but on the other, they are likely to gain some extra benefits. For example, communicating project objectives and outputs might become redundant because stakeholders will already be aware, many of them will already consider the initiatives their own, will become actively engaged in the project.

Participatory communication's value, however, is not only considered because of the better results it can yield. People's participation is also considered a right of its own by an increasing number of NGOs, international organizations and UN agencies.. In this respect participatory communication fulfils a broader social function, providing a voice to the poorest and the most marginalized of the people around the world. By engaging all relevant stakeholders, participatory communication becomes a tool that helps alleviate poverty, mitigates social exclusion, and ensures priorities and objectives are agreed to and refined by a wider base of the constituencies. This process enhances the overall results and sustainability of any development initiative.

Risks and constraints

When developing participatory approaches, there are some limitations and potential pitfalls to consider in regard to the quality and ownership of the interventions.

As to quality of interventions, Bill Cooke and Uma Khotari have drawn our attention to the "tyranny of the method" (Cooke and Khotari 2001). They address the risk of insisting on participatory strategy no matter what the context or the environment. With a growing consensus around the benefits of participatory strategies, a word of caution is called for as to the relevance, timeliness and content of proposed participatory strategies. Critiques of populist participatory approaches include the difficulty, if not impossibility, in managing a decision-making process with large numbers people involved speak to technical limitations and to theoretical, political and conceptual limitations in unfolding a participatory method. Inappropriate timing of participation (e.g., half-way through a project) can also lead to further delay and conflicts, especially when reverting to top-down approaches like trying to persuade people "to participate" in what has already been decided. In this respect, obstacles are sometimes unfairly ascribed to participation itself, rather than to its wrong application.

One condition for successful participatory approaches is the articulation of local ownership of the problem and related solution. Collective, community-based solutions are often the answer, yet in achieving these, there is the risk of "tyranny" of the group. Based on some myth of community in participatory approaches, "communities" often are seen by many practitioners as the turning point of bottom-up solutions. They are often taken for granted as homogeneous socio-economic and cultural entities– harmonious units where people share common lifestyles, interests and visions of life. In trying to emulate participation, it is important, however, not to conceal the power relations in a community, the differences in opinions, lifestyles, beliefs and the socio-economic distribution. A community can be full of tension, inequality and conflict, and practitioners need to be aware of the environment and treat the community as a sum of different groups rather than a homogeneous entity.

Finally a built-in problem exists in participatory approaches attempts to scale up the strategy. Given the differences among projects, their objectives and nature, and the host communities, replication is difficult. This is a risk to calculate with when strategies are defined and developed.

Different from one-way communication intervention, participatory communication requires a predominantly dialogic process, whose outcomes and implications are not always easy to pre-determine. This makes some managers of development initiatives uneasy. On the other hand, the higher the level of control from the top, the weaker the sense of ownership and commitment by the local stakeholders. Stakeholders' ownership and commitment are necessary ingredients to ensure better and more sustainable results.

Keywords: Genuine participation, dialogue, empowerment, project management, benefits, constraints

The Four Phases of the Communication Program Cycle

The communication program cycle can run parallel to the project cycle when they both start at the same time. As presented in Chapter 1, the basic phases of a communication program can be classified as:

- **Participatory Communication Assessment** (PCA) is where communication methods and tools are used to investigate and assess the situation;
- **(Participatory) Communication Strategy Design** is based on the findings of the research and defines the best way to apply communication to achieve the intended change;
- **Implementation of Communication Activities** to determine where activities planned in the previous phase are carried out;
- **Monitoring and Evaluation** runs through the whole communication program, monitoring progress and evaluating the final impact of the intervention.

To make the program cycle genuinely participatory, two-way communication should be adopted from the beginning and be applied consistently in each phase of the process. Because implementation success depends largely on the way the strategy has been designed, the first two phases, probing key issues and making decisions affecting the whole program, are crucial. Finally, monitoring and evaluation assesses progress and helps to make the necessary adjustments during the implementation and to measure the overall impact at the end. This classification is equally valid for outreach (one-way) types of communication programs, as well as for participatory (two-way) ones.

Full participation by all stakeholders in any step of the process is not possible and, in some cases probably not entirely desirable. For some situations and technical issues, it would not make sense to broaden the participatory decision-making exercise. If priorities are decided in a participatory manner and there is a broad consensus, for example, to build a bridge in a certain spot, there is no need to involve all stakeholders in the technical decisions concerning the type of concrete, bolts and other technical specifications for construction. Unless there are people familiar with different technical engineering specifications, general participation would only delay the process and would not benefit the end result. In general, however, an overall participatory process (at least in key steps) is relevant to ensure transparent leadership and management of a bridge or other infrastructure project, including securing equal access to the bridge according to agreed policies and pricing.

While allowing for stakeholders' participation, a development planner or project manager must balance inclusiveness with time, resources, interests and knowledge of individuals and groups related to the intended change. Key stakeholders affected by the change should have the opportunity to participate in the entire decision-making process defining the needed change. After their input is taken into account, however, they do not need to be directly involved in decisions, especially technical ones, that might go beyond their specific interest or knowledge. The next example should clarify this point.

Box 3.1. An Example of Participatory Communication Assessment

In a water project, officers of an international organization identified as a key development priority the need to improve the water system of a poor region in a Central American country. Based on their knowledge and expertise, the officials defined what was needed and which aspects should be improved, with little or no input from local stakeholders. Expectations of the stakeholders were not considered, and as problems emerged, project management came under increased pressure from the donor and national political authorities to gain the support of what are too often referred to as "beneficiaries." Thus, a more participatory stand was adopted in the following stages, and local stakeholders were involved in decisions concerning the technical design of the new water system.

The end results of this mixed approach (that is, top-down in the beginning and participatory from halfway mark) were less than satisfactory. Managers and a subsequent review mission ascribed much of the failure to participation, when in fact should have been ascribed to a faulty use of participatory communication. To be effective and actually participatory, the project should have sought participants' inputs at the beginning when assessing the situation and making decisions on what to do were made. Subsequent actions in the process could have been restricted to technical experts. This water project not only misused the concept of participation but also jeopardized the overall success of the project itself.

When stakeholders are not included from the start, participation is significantly impaired. In this example, local stakeholders should have been included in defining the needed outcome of the improved water system. They would have gained interest and been knowledgeable about which services were needed to improve lives. Rather they found themselves in a discussion of the technical design of a water system in which they had limited knowledge or interest. By switching these two basic factors—no stakeholder input in setting priorities and stakeholder inclusion in technical decisions—the project management set itself up for failure.

The Johari Window is a tool originally developed by Joseph Luft and Harry Inghman (hence the name) to explain interpersonal communication processes. It has been adapted to illustrate the dialogical process that exchanges knowledge and explores issues, leading to the best possible change. The Johari window is a useful tool to illustrate the process of joint decision making necessary in any participatory communication initiative. If "the unknown" is addressed successfully, the successful outcome is the definition of the objectives for the intended change. These objectives constitute the core of the subsequent communication strategy presented in the next pages.

Table 3.1 The Johari Window

Window 1: **OPEN KNOWLEDGE** What we know and they know	Window 3: **THEIR HIDDEN KNOWLEDGE** What they know and we do not know
Window 2: **OUR HIDDEN KNOWLEDGE** What we know and they do not know	Window 4: **THE BLIND SPOT** What neither we nor they know

Window #1 represents the first step of the initiative, starting with dialogue based on the common knowledge shared by all parties involved. "We" broadly refers to outside experts and project staff, while "They" refers to internal and local stakeholders. Window #2 represents knowledge of They, the local players, which is not known by the outside experts; window #3 is the opposite, knowledge of We, the outside experts, is shared with local stakeholders, covering areas not known to them. The final window represents the end of the exercise and concerns issue/s unknown to both groups. At this point knowledge, experiences, and skills of key stakeholders must come together to find the most appropriate options and solutions leading to the desired change. If key stakeholders jointly define the nature and extent of the intended change, the chances for success and sustainability of the initiative increase significantly.

Keywords: Communication program cycle, Johari window

Phase One: Participatory Communication Assessment (PCA)

In this phase, issues of relevance are researched and analyzed through two-way communication methods and techniques. For these tasks to be successful, it is necessary to establish an open or common space where key stakeholders can interact freely with each other. Establishing an open space facilitates the local stakeholder involvement in the decision-making process, thereby enhancing the chances of success and sustainability of the development initiative.

The name Participatory Communication Assessment (PCA) is derived from the Participatory Rural Communication Appraisal (PRCA) methodology created in the late 1990s. The PCRA was developed in Southern Africa by a joint FAO (Food and Agriculture Organizations of the United Nations)/SADC (Southern Africa Development Community) project based in Harare, Zimbabwe, as a way to enhance project design and operations (Anyaegbunam et al., 2004). As PCA, the name is partially modified and the concept is similar yet broader for two reasons: 1) to account for its wide range of applications reaching beyond the original rural focus and 2) to indicate the more analytical nature of this approach from the initial concept of appraisal to a more in-depth assessment of the situation, which usually includes options to address change and to seek solutions. PCA can be visualized as a funnel (figure 3.1), starting wide and narrowing down to define the key issues necessary to have a successful and sustainable change.

Some of the basic concepts and applications of PCA are also closely related other widely known participatory research methods, such as Participatory Rural Appraisal (PRA) and Participatory Action Research (PAR). Some of the principles of PCA are also applied in the communication-based assessment (CBA), an investigation method used by the Development Communication Division of the World Bank (Mefalopulos, 2008).

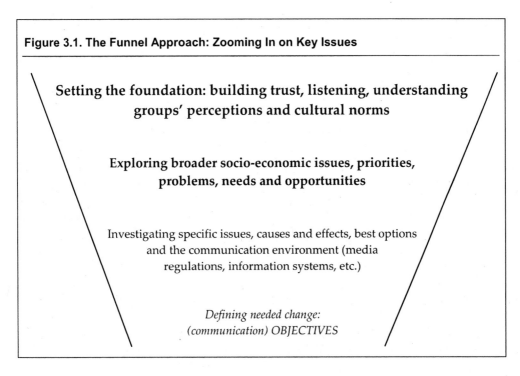

Figure 3.1. The Funnel Approach: Zooming In on Key Issues

Setting the foundation: building trust, listening, understanding groups' perceptions and cultural norms

Exploring broader socio-economic issues, priorities, problems, needs and opportunities

Investigating specific issues, causes and effects, best options and the communication environment (media regulations, information systems, etc.)

Defining needed change: (communication) OBJECTIVES

The following are basic steps in the PCA: 1) understand the socio-cultural context while identifying and defining key issues (including definition of key stakeholders); 2) create a common/public space, establish dialogue, and build trust among key stakeholders; 3) assess needs, problems, risks, opportunities, and solutions; 4) prioritize key issues for change and reconcile different perceptions; 5) validate findings and define solutions/objectives.

To clarify and simplify the adoption of participatory communication approaches, the following guidelines illustrate the steps to follow, as a general reference for practitioners. Variables such as experience in this approach, scope of the intervention and specific socio-cultural context may change the definition or sequence of the steps.

The scope of any development initiative is to improve the lives of some stakeholders. In the past, decisions on what change and how were left in the hands of a restricted group of decision makers and technical experts. More recently, such decisions increasingly involve key stakeholders. Nevertheless, often external actors continue to define a development project or program.

A classic example of external, top-down decision making

A group of agronomists manipulated crops that constituted the basic staple food for drought prone regions in parts of Africa. They produced a new plant with a shorter stem that required less water. The newly modified plant addressed the problem of water scarcity but the scientists did not contemplate another important issue. The long stems were used as building materials for roofs of huts, and therefore, the modified crop was abandoned after the initial adoption. This example is one among many where project innovations have failed to take into account local knowledge and needs, resulting in failure or underachievement.

The following steps indicate how to implement participatory communication-based research:

STEP 1: ISSUE IDENTIFICATION AND DEFINITION

Initiatives originate in a number of ways: request of local stakeholders, study by a public or private organization, government-defined priority or need identified by outside technical experts. Whatever the origin, a participatory communication assessment adopted initially to explore all relevant issues is most effective.

The use of the participatory communication assessment at the beginning is *exploratory*: it is not restricted to a specific area or sector but is open to all areas and issues deemed relevant by one of various stakeholder groups. Conversely a PCA adopted in an on-going project with objectives already set is *topical*: it is restricted to investigate and probe topics related to set objectives. In this case, topical PCA should be considered a partial participatory approach, since the main priorities/objectives are already defined, and probably not in a participatory way.

To be genuinely exploratory, a PCA should assess any issue deemed important by stakeholders, including issues of global import such as climate change. It will be essentially exploratory since the PCA can investigate and explore various key issues, risks, and perceptions, and come up with key priorities and recommendations within a broad spectrum of applications.

On the other hand, there is the example of a project with the main goal to reduce the environmental impact of the destruction of the Amazon forest. The project manager may request a communication intervention in order to find ways to stop the practice of starting fires (even though often farmers are not the major cause of such problems), which lead to significant forest destruction. In order to design an effective communication strategy a PCA will need to investigate the causes of the fires and probe farmers' perceptions and rationale for starting those fires. Even if topical, to be at least partially participatory, the findings of the PCA will need to be discussed and negotiated with project management. If it is not, the whole exercise will be reduced to a top-down, one-way persuasion initiative, which is highly questionable not only from a participatory perspective but also as far as results are concerned.

Clearly, the range of a topical participatory communication assessment is limited by the boundaries set by the project nature and objectives. Therefore, if the objectives are set properly and are considered relevant by key stakeholders, PCA can still play a major role in the overall success of the initiative. If this is not the case, the major contribution of PCA should be to identify critical areas, obstacles and risks, feeding these findings back to project management.

When defining the area of intervention it is also crucial to identify and engage the major stakeholders and their basic positions and perceptions about the proposed change as soon as possible. All the key issues and the various stakeholders' perspectives will be investigated and probed further during the next steps.

STEP 2: ESTABLISH A COMMON SPACE

This step is often neglected, yet it is one of the most crucial. Past experiences teaches that many project failures result from two major factors: faulty project design and lack of buy-in by those who are supposed to be beneficiaries. Both of these problems are due to a basic flaw: insufficient or very limited involvement of key stakeholders in the decision-making process of the development initiative. Establishing a space where all stakeholders feel comfortable enough to express their views, share their concerns, and provide their inputs on the desired change is key for the success and long-term sustainability of any initiative. This step, when adopted, comes after the initial definition of issue/s of interest and is the ideal one to start any initiative.

Key stakeholders must interact, achieve a mutual understanding, and then seek a consensus about priorities.[2] All of this can be achieved only if all parties trust and talk to each other. Building trust is, therefore, a very important prerequisite to ensure genuine participatory communication. Creating a common space can engender this trust. The space can be established in many ways, such as regular meetings in a physical space open to everybody, more formal mechanisms where stakeholder representatives convene and engage in a dialogue facilitated by a neutral source, or where appropriate, use of interactive technologies, such as the internet, to allow people no matter how distant to provide their inputs and interact directly with the other players.

There are a number of communication methods, techniques and icebreakers, which are particularly effective in establishing trust and require a high degree of empathy and understanding of the situation. These tools include a *transect walk* in rural and peri-urban settings where local stakeholders walk around the community illustrating the various social and productive areas to outsiders; *historical timeline* to trace the history and patterns of certain populations; *trend lines* to identify if and when certain phenomena (such as AIDS, soil erosion, and so forth) have occurred, making it easier to identify key causes and possible solutions; and *seasonal/daily calendar* in which relevant groups describe key activities during the different time of the years, or even daily activities, according to the scope of the investigation.

0All of these are dialogic tools, using two-way communication. Outside experts should act as facilitators to make certain that dialogue, while covering key areas, flows freely in directions considered important by stakeholders. When these activities have established trust and issues of interest are jointly explored, it is possible to proceed to the next step.

STEP 3: ASSESSING NEEDS, PROBLEMS, RISKS, OPPORTUNITIES, AND SOLUTIONS

From this point the investigation focuses on areas related to the agreed change. Two-way communication explores areas of interest, regardless of the sector, which can include environment, governance, health, infrastructure, agriculture or any other initiative-related area. Participatory communication assesses relevant problems, risks and needs and it identifies best options, opportunities and solutions. Participatory communication is the key for the discovery process, described previously in the Johari window, acknowledging what each party knows and does not know, facilitating the sharing of existing knowledge, creating new knowledge and defining solutions to achieve the intended change.

A number of methods and tools can be used to investigate issues of relevance. A *baseline study* is a valuable tool to implement at the beginning of the communication initiative, before the situation is changed. The baseline has two functions: 1) measuring the situation at the beginning of the communication intervention, in order to evaluate its overall impact in an accurate manner by comparing the findings with a second study carried out at the end of the initiative; and 2) validating and quantifying the extent of the initial findings defined through qualitative methods. For instance, if a few ad-hoc interviews reveal that there are some reservations about the proposed change to give more political and financial power to local authorities, a baseline study can further probe the reasons for these positions and quantify how widespread are these views among other stakeholders.

One of the most common techniques is *the problem tree*. It starts from a problem or undesired situation (graphically represented by the trunk of the tree) draws an in-depth picture of the overall situation, investigating the causes (the roots of the tree) and the effects (the branches of the tree). Often another technique is used in conjunction, *the solution tree*. It follows the same logic, however, instead of going deeper into problem-analysis, it uses the logical framework to focus on available options and best solutions.

One-to-one interviews and *focus groups* are among the most frequently used methods of investigating key issues. Although not necessarily genuinely participatory techniques, however, if conducted properly they can be part of a participatory process. A *focus group* is usually composed of eight to ten individuals with a common relationship to the issue probed. For instance, women of reproductive age can form a focus group probing perceptions of birth control methods or farmers of different ages and genders could form a group exploring the introduction of innovative techniques in agriculture.

In rural settings, *community resource mapping* is a useful tool that allows communities, even the illiterate ones, to describe their major source of income. *Livelihood mapping* is a similar tool, but its focus is more on people's occupation rather than on the overall resources of community. *Social maps* can provide a wider understanding of the social composition of a community, which are seldom homogeneous entities. These techniques can be used sequentially to validate results and to reach a better understanding of the socio-economic structure of a community or groups of stakeholders.

Communication-related issues. When dealing with communication-related issues, a number of techniques are used: communication resource mapping indicates in which way communities and stakeholders communicate among themselves and their preferred channels of information; Venn diagrams are useful to assess the influence of various actors and institutions and the way information flows among them; and a media environment audit investigates existing media infrastructure and current legislation on media.

When dealing with communication issues, it is important not only to identify formal and institutional channels but also the informal ones, which are often more important than the others. This identification is even more relevant in monologic approaches. For instance, while officers of the Ministry of Agriculture can play a valuable role in introducing an innovation of a certain harvesting technique, a successful farmer in the area could be even more influential in persuading[3] farmers to adopt the innovation. A project in Eastern Africa, despite the use of key institutional figures and city doctors, experienced many problems in having villagers adopt a practice that could prevent many illnesses. Success came only when local community healers were taken on board and became key channels of persuasion for people to adopt the new practice.

STEP 4: PRIORITIZE KEY ISSUES FOR CHANGE AND RECONCILE DIFFERENT PERCEPTIONS

After investigating key issues, assessing problems, causes and risks, and identifying options and opportunities, it is important to probe and triangulate the findings. This determines if the issues are perceived and considered equally important by all key stakeholders. Even when there is a broad consensus on a problem, there may be many different views on how to address it. As a result analysis of the causes of the problem is needed to prioritize the various reasons and their solutions

For instance, to effectively devise a communication strategy it is not enough to know that the key problem is the destruction of the forest in a region, nor is it enough to know if the farmers start the fires when clearing their fields. To devise a strategy to reduce or eliminate this problem, it is necessary to know if the forest is burned intentionally or mostly due to careless acts. The farmers' perceptions about the forest are also important. Do they see the forest as a resource for future generations or as an impediment for the expansion of their fields? This and other issues need to be assessed, contrasted and ranked among the various stakeholders' groups.

Once a restricted set of priorities, problems or needs is defined, the list can be reconciled with different perceptions among the various groups, using a number of tools. *The window of perceptions* is a technique devised to compare and contrast different perspectives even in complex projects. It requires drawing a diagram of the key issue and how the different stakeholders' groups perceive its causes and effects. The various diagrams are then compared and when significant divergences are identified, two-way communication is used to reconcile those differences.

In instances where a straightforward comparison among different items is required (e.g., probing top health risks as perceived by a community) there are other simpler tools to be used. *Pair wise preference ranking* is a technique to probe stakeholders' views and rank a set of issues in any sector such as health, agriculture or infrastructure. Its goal is to allow stakeholders to express their opinions about which issues are more important. It is particularly useful when trying to understand and weigh causes of problems and potential conflicts.

As the participatory communication assessment unfolds and different perceptions and positions emerge, dialogue should be used to facilitate understanding of differences and common ground and to reconcile the various views.

STEP 5: VALIDATE FINDINGS AND DEFINE SOLUTIONS/OBJECTIVES

Once all the issues of interest have been investigated, priorities defined and best course of action agreed upon, the final part of the Participatory Communication Assessment can take place. It requires careful synthetic and analytical skills, since the amount of data collected for interpretation is often extensive. Findings must also be compared and contrasted across the whole spectrum of relevant stakeholders, because the communication specialist's main task should be that of interpreting stakeholders' inputs and identifying patterns leading to a change agreed by most. Combining a careful diagnosis with the logical process of problem solving derives this wider consensus, making the definition of objectives more relevant to stakeholders.

The role of the communication specialist at this point is to interpret the information collected and facilitate the definition of the path with the better options. Some creative thinking is often needed to ensure a broad consensus among stakeholders and define the best solution. Any PCA should end up with the identification and definition of the objective/s of the development project or program. This is the most critical part of any program, but even more so one based on participatory principles. There cannot be genuine participation if stakeholders do not take part in the decision-making process to define the scope of change and the objectives through which to achieve it.

The genuine use of participatory communication facilitates a collaborative working mode among stakeholders, allowing the sharing of different experiences and knowledge. This enhances the problem-analysis and problem-solving processes, leading to the definition of the objectives of the initiative. Proper identification and analysis of the causes behind an undesired situation are the most important factors in a successful definition of the objectives needed to achieve the desired change.

Keywords: Participatory Rural Communication Appraisal (PRCA); Participatory Rural Appraisal (PRA); Participatory Action Research (PAR), Participatory Communication Assessment (PCA), exploratory assessment, topical assessment.

Phase Two: (Participatory) Communication Strategy Design

Any successful design of a communication strategy, or any strategy, begins with the definition of the objectives. This might seem an obvious statement, yet instances where strategies are designed on broad, shaky and even poorly understood objectives are more frequent than expected. When this happens, crisis and failures become the norm.

For example, in a poverty reduction program one of the objectives was to promote sustainable livelihoods of communities in rural areas. The objectives were so vague and broad that they allowed for a large number of possible interpretations and course of actions. As a result, the communication strategy was weak and it was difficult for the communication specialist to determine what was conceived and understood by "sustainable livelihoods." Notably, even the conception of poverty reduction was a source of trouble and confusion. The way poverty was defined by the donor and the implementing agency was not accepted by local communities—many of whom refused to be labelled as poor. The local communities boycotted many of the activities that were intended and defined for the "poor."

Similar to the first phase, a series of basic steps can help understand how to design a communication strategy based on a participatory communication assessment, helping to avoid problems of vague intent. Full participation of stakeholders in all steps is not an imperative as long as key decisions take stakeholders' inputs into account and/or are validated with stakeholders at a later stage. For instance, a communication specialist can design a radio or television message to raise awareness of avian flu provided that the avian flu issue has been first introduced and positioned with key stakeholders. To ensure a proper strategy design, the specialist also needs to be familiar with audiences' knowledge, culture, perceptions and priorities.

Design of a participatory communication strategy divides into two broad modalities: monologic and dialogic. Monologic, a one-way communication approach, promotes, for example, a public reform, raising awareness of innovation that can benefit stakeholders or designing a health campaign to promote a desired behavior. The level of change addressed by this approach concerns one or a mix of the following: awareness, knowledge, attitudes or behaviours, and practices.

Not everybody might agree to include one-way approaches within the context of participatory communication, however, participation is not an absolute concept— either there or not. Participation does not always mean everybody is engaged in every step of the way. It can also be considered as a way to ensure the opportunity for stakeholders to participate in key steps of the decision-making process. Bella Mody (1991) refers to participatory message design, based on audiences' inputs, as a most effective way to design and implement campaigns: this implementation through mass media can be considered mainly one-way.

The second modality, dialogic, concerns strategies requiring a change in the level of collaboration, mediation, conflict resolution, mobilization or partnership, and coalition building. Participatory communication can enhance social accountability and transparency in the growing sector of good governance, which promotes the establishment of common spaces where various constituencies meet to air and negotiate different positions.

In Chapter 1, the distinctions between the dialogic and monologic modalities were introduced in the heuristic framework for communication for development at the conceptual level. In Chapter 2, they were further fleshed out through ten guiding questions and served as guidance for the elaboration of participatory communication strategies. The following elaborates on both modalities of communication.

In a monologic modality the basic steps of strategy design are to define 1) SMART objective/s (SMART stands for specific, measurable, achievable, relevant, time-bound); 2) primary and secondary audience; 3) level/type of change (i.e., awareness, knowledge, attitude, or behavior); 4) communication approaches and activities; 5) channels and media; 6) messages; 7) expected outputs and/or outcomes.

In a dialogic modality the steps do not differ significantly. The major difference is that change is not rigidly predefined, but the result of the interaction among the various stakeholders. The basic steps are to define 1) SMART objectives; 2) stakeholders; 3) level/type of change (e.g., collaboration, mobilization, mediation, partnership building, etc.); 4) communication approaches and activities; 5) partners, channels and, eventually, venues; 6) target issues; 7) expected outputs and/or outcomes.

Hence, the main differences reside in a couple of steps. In step two, audiences in the monologic mode are substituted by the more active conception of stakeholders in the dialogic mode. In the third step, the level of expected change differs: in the monologic mode it usually refers to a change in awareness, knowledge, attitudes, practices or behaviors, while in the dialogic mode it can refer to the level of trust, collaboration or partnership established, or even to the outcome of a joint investigation and analysis. In the following section, the steps of strategy design for each of the two modalities are illustrated through practical examples.

An example of the monologic modality of communication.

Clearly an example in this modality can only have limited degree of participation. In this case the example refers to a rural development project in Latin America and the issue of climate change. The participatory communication assessment identified a number of issues to address; one seemed particularly important: soil degradation caused by a number of factors, including the poor use of land by farmers. The main effects of soil degradation reduced the productivity of the land, increased the risk of landslide in the rainy season, and had a negative environmental impact due to the gradual reduction of the forest.

One of the project priorities was to raise the awareness of local farmers about the negative effects of soil degradation while enhancing their knowledge and capacities on how to use land in a more sustainable way. Even if the communication objectives (addressing change in the awareness and knowledge level) point to a strategy based on a one-way, monologic modality, the overall approach can still be considered within the participatory communication boundaries, although to a limited degree, since the strategy was derived through a participatory communication assessment and stakeholders inputs were taken into account throughout the process.

STEP 1: TAKE IDENTIFIED OBJECTIVES AND TRANSFORM TO SMART OBJECTIVES

The SMART requirements can be considered as guidelines to define objectives in a feasible and measurable manner. In this instance the two objectives can be made SMART in the following way: objective #1 raise awareness to 80 percent of local farmers on the negative consequences of soil erosion by the project end; and objective #2) ensure that 70 percent of local farmers know and can apply basic agricultural techniques, allowing a sustainable use of land in agriculture by a set date. These quantitative outcomes should be based on the existing data, which can be provided by a baseline study.

It should be noted how in the proposed objectives the purpose is to raise awareness and increase knowledge, and not to have farmers adopt the new practices, even if that is the eventual project aim. It is therefore important that the indicators and the subsequent impact evaluation in the first phase will focus on these two factors (i.e., change in awareness and knowledge) rather than in a change in practices or behaviors.

STEP 2: INCLUDE NEEDED INFORMATION ABOUT AUDIENCES

To illustrate the basic steps in designing a monologic communication strategy, focus on the first objective, raising awareness. It is clear the primary audiences are the farmers, however, a number of secondary audiences can be identified who influence farmers and raise their awareness about soil degradation. Among them are teachers, who influence students, who in turn can in turn influence the parents/farmers, and the extension agents, who with proper training and tools can become important channels to raise farmer awareness.

STEP 3: DEFINE THE INTENDED LEVEL OF CHANGE TO ACHIEVE

In this case the objective indicates the intended change is awareness and knowledge level. The rationale for explicitly defining the level or type of change is to keep the design of the intervention and the related activities focused on target objectives; hence on the needed change.

STEP 4: FOUR DEFINE COMMUNICATION APPROACHES AND/OR ACTIVITIES TO EFFECTIVELY ACHIEVE THE OBJECTIVE

In this case an effective objective would be to raise the farmers' awareness of the implications of soil erosion. If social marketing is considered to be an effective approach in the context, it will provide the broader framework within which the communication activities are selected. Radio ads and talk shows, public meetings, posters and regular meetings with extensionists can be some of the activities to raise farmers' awareness. Each decision, however, depends on the resources available and the knowledge of the local context acquired during the PCA.

STEP 5: SELECT THE MOST APPROPRIATE AND EFFECTIVE MEDIA AND CHANNELS TO ACHIEVE THE INTENDED OBJECTIVE

Step 5 is closely intertwined with the previous step. In this case, radio, print materials in the form of posters, meetings, extensionists and teachers[4] have been identified as proper channels. Some degree of overlapping between one step and another should not be considered as duplication, since it can provide useful triangulation and validation of previous decisions and insights.

STEP 6: DESIGN THE MESSAGE TO RAISE AWARENESS LEVELS

Step 6concerns the design of messages to raise the awareness level of farmers. To be effective the message design should be derived from the findings of the participatory communication assessment. In this instance, the PCA had revealed that most farmers did not associate the catastrophic effects of mudslides with cultivation techniques that caused or reinforced soil erosion. Once this fact was probed and confirmed, a series of messages linking the elements was designed and successfully increased farmers' awareness through a multimedia campaign, including radio, posters, and interpersonal methods.

STEP 7: CONSIDER THE EXPECTED OUTCOMES

Step 7 can be factored in at a later stage. Considering this step as part of the communication strategy, however, keeps the strategy focused on the expected change, while also considering how to assess and measure it. In this case, the expected outcome is straightforward—the level of change in farmers' awareness—but in many other cases it is not. Moreover, the difference between outputs and outcomes should always be kept in mind. Output refers to the immediate result, usually quantitative, of an activity, while outcome refers to how the activities impact the desired change. For instance the output of a training workshop can be the number of people trained, while the outcome concerns whether the skills acquired have been applied and with what result.

An example of the Dialogic modality of communication

An example of water sector reform, related to the broader framework of good governance, can be used to illustrate the steps to design an effective communication strategy in the dialogic mode. The broad objective was to improve water services, which were considered inefficient and with little or no accountability mechanisms to protect consumers' inputs.

STEP 1: DEFINE THE KEY PRIORITY

Step 1 as derived by the PCA defines a key priority for improving water services as the establishment of mechanisms to ensure citizens input and feedback in the system. Among the identified SMART objectives, the one used in this case is the establishment of a partnership among the main actors in order to ensure accountability and transparency in the system.

The main actors involved are 1) the local water utilities, private companies responsible for providing water services to consumers; 2) regional water boards, which respond to the Ministry of Natural Resources and are responsible to maintain the good condition and satisfactory service of the water infrastructure; and the 3) water consumers group, which represent the interests of the consumers. The experience and related literature confirm that in a dialogic mode, it is harder to have fully SMART objectives, as change requiring collaboration, mediation or partnership building are harder to quantify and accurately evaluate than changes in level of awareness, knowledge or behaviors.

STEP 2: DEFINE THE RELEVANT ACTORS

Similarly to the previous strategy, in step 2 the stated objective already defines the actors of relevance, or stakeholders, who are named in this context. The definition of these groups, (local water utilities, regional water boards and water consumer groups) including an understanding of the composition and functions of each group, is all that is required in this step.

STEP 3. FIGURE OUT THE SCOPE OF THE STRATEGY

Step three is the level of change or the scope of the strategy, and in this case, it refers to establishing a partnership to improve the situation. Achieving this task could be harder than expected since good intentions by the stakeholders directly engaged in the meetings might not be enough. Institutional buy-in is also needed to guarantee support and sustainability to the partnership, particularly through difficult times. On the supply side (water utilities and water boards) the institutional buy-in must be validated by the top management, while on the demand side (consumers) the fact that consumers pay for water services should ensure their interest and commitment. Thus it is in consumers' interest to ensure water services are delivered effectively and efficiently.

STEP 4: SELECT THE COMMUNICATION APPROACHES AND/OR ACTIVITIES TO ACHIEVE THE SET OBJECTIVE

In this case, the activities identified first are the drafting of a memorandum of understanding about roles, duties and responsibilities for each of the three parties, a calendar of regular meetings and clear two-way reporting lines. Representatives of the water utilities have to report on issues that emerge in the partnership meetings to their management and then back to the other partners. The representatives of the water boards need to report to their Ministry and then report back to the partners on any decisions taken. Finally, the consumer representatives have to inform consumers of decisions and actions taken in response to their suggestions and complaints, while at the same time making sure to have open channels to collect consumer feedback in a timely manner.

STEP 5: DEFINE PARTNERS AND CHANNELS

Once the activities are established, an effective *modus operandi* for the partnership has been identified, step 5 defines partners and channels. Due to the nature of the original objective (i.e., establishing a partnership) the partners here are the representatives of the three stakeholders' groups already defined in *step two*: local water utilities, regional water board and water consumers groups. In a similar way, the channels are defined in *step four* and are mainly meetings, followed by reporting to their respective audiences.

STEP 6 REFINE AND ADDRESS KEY ISSUES

These need to be discussed to share and understand each others' points of view and seek solutions that are within the framework established in the beginning, reconciling different interests and responsibilities. Due to the diversity of the issues and openness of the process is not often easy to predefine the content of what will be discussed in great detail, but it is usually possible to frame the broader issues, also based on the feedback provided by each partner.

STEP 7 CONSIDER THE EXPECTED OUTCOMES

Finally, step 7 requires the definition of what is expected once the strategy is implemented successfully. Clearly the outcome of such an initiative, which is more genuinely participatory,[5] is also more difficult to define accurately than in the previous example, which aimed to increase awareness. In this instance the expected change relates to the establishment of a working partnership among the three key players with the outcome emerging from the partnership. The evaluation then should assess both how well the three parties are able to collaborate and what results are produced by such collaboration.

Each of the two strategy templates presented here, monologic and dialogic, follow a similar pattern. When adopting a dialogic modality, however, the initiative is clearly more participatory and requires a higher degree of flexibility to adapt to multi-party outcomes, which are not always easy to predict. To be successfully and genuinely applied, dialogue and two-way communication not only require adoption from the beginning but also require a strong commitment and a high degree of ethical standards by the facilitators.

Paulo Freire once stated, "Dialogue cannot exist, however, in the absence of a profound love for the world and for the people. The naming of the world, which is an act of creation and re-creation, is not possible if it is not infused with love.... Because love is an act of courage, and not of fear, love is commitment to others" (Freire 1997: 70). Such a statement may appear too idealistic to some readers. It does help, however, to explain better what many consider one of the major underlying factors that drive participatory approaches—the passion and commitment that goes beyond the purely professional competencies.

Keywords: Communication strategy design, SMART objectives, monologic communication, dialogic communication.

Phase Three: Implementation of Communication Activities

Once the communication strategy has been defined, it is important to draw an action plan to implement and facilitate the management and monitoring of all relevant activities. There are many possible ways to devise and organize an action plan. Table 3.2, which refers to the example in section 3.4, presents a sample action plan.

Starting from the objective, the plan includes people (audiences or stakeholders) who are engaged in the needed change, activities planned, resources needed (human and financial), party responsible for each activity, and timeframe. Finally a column about the indicators to assess outputs and outcomes can also be added to facilitate the monitoring of the activities.

If the strategy is designed properly, most of the activities in the action plan are defined in a straightforward and logical way. Based on the findings of the PCA, some decisions require a mix of professional skills and creative insights, as every situation is different and takes place in a unique cultural and social setting. For example, avian flu prevention projects have as objectives to alert people and to engage them in discussing and implementing preventive actions to minimize threats, especially in rural areas.

Table 3.2. Communication Action Plan

Objective: Raise the awareness of the negative consequences of soil erosion to 80% of local farmers

Audience/ stakeholders	Activities	Resources	Party responsible	Timeframe	Indicators
Who are the actors addressed by the initiative	Which are the needed activities?	What are the financial/human resources needed?	Who is the party (person or institution) responsible?	What is the schedule for their completion?	Which are the indicators to assess and evaluate their impact?
Local farmers	Production of radio programs, posters and training workshops	Funding for design and production of radio programs and posters, and for training courses	Extension unit in the Ministry of Agriculture	End of 2009	Surveys indicating level of awareness of farmers on the given topic

In Latin America, community radio is a popular medium in many regions of the continent and would be advisable as a main channel. In many parts of Africa given its tradition and broad diffusion, popular theatre could provide a better approach to engage local communities.

The strategy and the related action plan must always take into account the context, the resources available and any other factor that might affect the implementation of the activities. The indicators column signals that monitoring and evaluation should be a consideration throughout the whole intervention, even if the final assessment is done after its completion.

Keywords: communication action plan

Phase Four: Monitoring and Evaluation

In many instances, this evaluation phase is planned and performed only toward the end of a project, while in reality, its planning should start at the beginning of an initiative. Furthermore, in a genuine participatory communication modality, the usual approach of assigning the responsibility of the design and implementation of the evaluation to external experts cannot be considered a proper course of action. If participation means that stakeholders are partners in the decision-making process, it follows logically that they must also be partners in the process of evaluating the impact of that change.

Too often the evaluation of communication activities is focused on outputs (for example, materials produced, number of viewers reached or number of staff trained) or on technical aspects (such as rate and use of innovations, adoption of new behaviors). Usually neglected are consideration of stakeholder satisfaction and feedback about the proposed change. To be participatory, decisions on what and how to assess change must be agreed jointly by all key stakeholders. For instance, when measuring the impact of an innovation, quantitative methods, rooted in a scientific methodology and often required by international organizations, can be used in conjunction with more qualitative methods. Not always considered as "scientific," qualitative measures assess the level of satisfaction and opinions of the ultimate users at the local level. Dialogue can help reconcile the different positions and needs, making sure that all stakeholders' inputs are considered.

For example, participatory communication articulates social change processes where monitoring the actual process is crucial to understand the outcomes. Figueroa identified seven key process indicators of social change: leadership, degree of equity of participation, information equity, collective self-efficacy, sense of ownership, social cohesion and social norms (Figueroa and others, 2002). Figueroa's methodology was as an attempt to quantify the changes occurring, thus seeking to numerically "weigh" the change. This is a difficult task, as the indicators are seeking to capture social change processes. Similarly, qualitative methodologies have been developed, for instance, the increasingly popular "Most Significant Change" methodology. It is based on the principle of systematically assessing and analytically synthesizing stories of change narrated by the participating people.

In the current structure of development, however, based on projects and programs planned and managed by outside entities, genuine participatory evaluation is difficult to adopt, given tight deadlines and rigid reporting lines. Nonetheless, this approach increasingly being used in small-scale, community-driven development initiatives. When success in these types of projects can be documented in a systematic way, it will become easier to promote and scale-up genuine participatory communication evaluation approaches in bigger initiatives.

In conclusion, it should be emphasized that while impact evaluation is conducted at the end of the communication initiative, it needs to be planned from the very beginning of the initial phase. If indicators are not defined, validated and assessed from the start, no measurement will be able to assess the impact of the initiative after its activities are implemented. The same holds true for monitoring indicators that are needed to ensure that the planning and implementation of the activities stay on track.

Keywords: Monitoring indicators, evaluation indicators

Notes

[1] It should be noted that the terms "genuine dialogue" and "genuine participation" indicate the highest possible form of dialogue, that is an open and balanced communication flow among all parties, and the form of participation where all parties have an equal opportunity to participate and affect the decision-making process.

[2] The authors are aware to walk a thin line here, since genuine participatory communication approaches are not fully compatible with the rigid structures of current conception of development initiatives that requires tight and timely outputs, usually defined well in advance.

[3] Once more, persuasion does not need to be considered exclusively as a one-way, top-down effort, but it can also be a way to seek for better options in a dialogue among two or more parties (Mefalopulos, 2008).

[4] Note that while extensionists and teachers are stakeholders, they can also become channels in some of the activities of the overall communication strategy.

[5] Again, genuinely participatory refers to a higher level of participation, as defined previously in this publication, with the higher level of difficulty in accurately measuring its outcome.

CHAPTER 4

Participatory Communication in Civil Society

This chapter presents three cases to illustrate how civil society organizations approach participatory communication. The cases illustrate different contextual factors to consider, including culture, socio-economic conditions, and policy. These cases illustrate that when civil society practices participatory communication processes, they move beyond the project focus outlined in Chapter 3. All three cases presented are part of longer term societal processes, engaging in the pursuit of long-term objectives of empowerment while organizing in donor-funded project cycles of 3-5 years.

Women, Healthy Lifestyles and Community Empowerment

Minga Peru is a non-profit, community-based organization working with communication for social change. It was established in 1998 by a Peruvian couple who worked as social communicators in the Peruvian Amazon region. The aim of Minga Peru is community development to address issues of social justice, gender equity, reproductive health, and human rights. Its main group of interest is the women of the region, although they also work with their families, and increasingly have worked with the men.

Peru's northern Loreto region is inhabited by indigenous groups—over 65 linguistic groups representing over 13 main ethnic groups. It is the poorest region of Peru with widespread problems of unemployment, a broad range of poverty-related health problems (like malnourishment, high infant mortality, sexually transmitted infections, etc.) and a series of social problems like domestic violence and very high fertility rates. The region is a river plateau with a very dispersed population. Although Loreto covers one third of the Peruvian territory, only 5 percent of the nation's population lives in the area. Thus, radio becomes a useful medium to reach this very dispersed population.

Minga's strategy in Loreto region is to support the development of "communicative spaces," which stimulate a culture of participation and public debate. Consequently the local community members are empowered to take an active part in the development of their local community. Minga Peru gives particular attention to issues of cultural diversity and gender inequality.

In order to pursue their objectives, Minga has three core activities:

1. Production of a 30-minute radio program *Bienvenida Salud* (Welcome Health), which is transmitted three times a week via five radio stations in the region, reaching 80 percent of the region's inhabitants. Almost 500 episodes have been produced in the first eight years. With re-transmission, 1,100 broadcasts have aired and reached the most remote areas of the Loreto region (Sengupta 2007).

2. A "Community Empowerment and Leadership Program" is a training program for community health workers (*promotoras*), in which women from the region are educated in basic human, sexual, and reproductive rights, self esteem and preventive health care. By participating in a training session every third month at Minga Peru's training center, the women achieve technical skills, have social network opportunities with each other, and engage in a process of empowerment. Today, many of these approximately 500 women are important catalysts in local community development processes throughout the small, dispersed communities in the region.

3. Support of income generating activities is another activity whereby women can gain economic independence and a more active role in local community development. By providing women with economic opportunities, Minga directly challenges the traditional gender structures and the economic dependency of women upon men. At the same time, it offers households possibilities for real economic development.

At the center of Minga Peru's participatory communication strategy lays a deep recognition of cultural diversity, socio-economic realism and gendered power struggles in the families and communities. Guiding their holistic approach, where radio broadcasting, income generating activities, social networking and capacity building are integrated into a joint strategy, lies principles of plurality of voice, horizontal communication and dialogue, bottom-up communication and active community participation in the mediated public sphere. These elements permeate the different stages of Minga Peru's activities as working principles.

Participatory Communication in Minga, Peru

Participatory communication is embedded in the whole design of a Minga, Peru project. Their strong community-based approach is illustrated through many elements:

- Active encouragement from Minga for community radio listeners to send letters to the editorial team of *Bienvenida Salud*. This has resulted in more than 6000 letters sent from 1998-2007, many having direct impact on the development of scripts for the radio drama, as well as on the topics for discussion in the radio program. Minga articulates cultural sensitivity, recognizes cultural diversity and incorporates this understanding into the radio drama, which produces a strong cultural connectivity and a firm base for widespread identification and engagement around the characters.
- The use of youth correspondents from the communities has secured a strong connection between community experiences and issues addressed on the

radio. This provides the communities with access to and voice within radio broadcasting.

■ The emphasis on social networking and its integration with capacity building programs has resulted in a stronger social cohesion within the region. The network of community health workers across the Loreto region has become a strong element in the promotion of healthy lifestyles.

One of the most prominent outcomes detected in the Minga, Peru initiative lies in the empowerment of women. They have gained self-confidence and begun a more articulate participation in the public sphere. Women have also developed stronger social and professional networks and have improved their capacity to handle the health challenges of the region. This has not only improved the quality of the health care but also has developed a broader rights-based approach to health in the region.

The Minga Peru project draws on both the monologic and dialogic communication practices outlined in Chapter 2. Emphasis is on monologic communication practices to transmit and disseminate relevant information to the community, drawing on the participatory production practices of radio programming. Emphasis, however, is also on a conscious effort to work toward the longer-term empowerment of women and youth in these Amazon communities.

> **Keywords**: Holistic and bottom-up approach, rights-based community development. Participatory script development; integrated social networking and capacity building component. Empowerment through active participation in communication practices.

Youth and Participatory Governance

Femina HIP (Health Information Project) is a Tanzanian NGO, founded in 1999. It has grown continuously, and today has 30 employees and a broad range of interconnected communication activities. Entertainment education is its primary communication strategy to engage youth in the Tanzanian development process. Femina HIP is a multi-media initiative grounded in principles of participatory communication. Femina articulates its own media platform in the intersection between radio programs, television programs, large print media, schools clubs, community outreach programs, and a web portal. Their objective is to build supportive environments in Tanzania where the following can occur:

■ The ability of young people to enjoy in their own communities their right to access information and services leading to healthy lifestyles, and to be empowered to make positive, informed choices on sexuality in order to reduce the negative impact of HIV/AIDS.

■ The ability for communities to exercise their right to express themselves, participate in public debate and engage in civil society. (Femina HIP Logical Framework, 2007)

These stated objectives affirm a mission to deliver information and services, as well as pursue advocacy to empower communities in general and youth in particular to make informed choices. An additional goal is personal empowerment whereby community members learn to express themselves, participate in public debate, and engage in civil society.

The objectives of Femina are met through a broad range of communication activities and synergies, guided by five-year strategic plan (2006-2010). The core activities of Femina include two large magazines: *FEMA*, addressing primarily urban youth, and *SiMchezo!*, addressing the rural population. In addition, Femina is involved in a radio soap opera, an interactive television talk show, an interactive website and a broad range of individual publications (see box 4.1 for details). Distribution and use of the print materials is through partnerships with approximately 200 NGOs and CBOs.

Femina HIP has established itself as an NGO with a relatively strong presence in the media and with a broad constituency among the low-income populations of Tanzania. Compared with the actual mass media and the leading mainstream radio, television, and print media, Femina HIP is not big. As a civil society-driven media platform, however, they are among the largest.

The organization operates at multiple levels of intervention:

- At the individual and family level, Femina HIP works on a) production and accessibility of relevant information for their readers and viewers; b) opening channels for dialogue and debate. One of their unique forums for dialogue is the use of SMS as a response mechanism for individuals watching their television talk show.
- At the community level, Femina HIP works to strengthen youth participation around issues of concern by supporting Femina Clubs hosted at secondary schools. Some of these clubs have evolved into independent CBOs with their own space to meet and their own community-based work plans.

Box 4.1. Femina Media Outlets

FEMA – A glossy magazine of 64 pages published four times a year with a run of 120,000 copies, which will rise to 170,000 copies per quarter by the end of 2008. Intended for youth aged 15-24, especially secondary school students in every region of the country.

SiMchezo! – A magazine of 32 pages published six times a year with a run of 140,000 copies, which will rise to 250,000 copies each issue by the end of 2008. Intended for out of school youth and their communities, particularly in rural areas.

Pilika Pilika – A radio soap opera produced by the NGO "Mediae," carrying messages from Femina, as well as two other organizations. Airs on national radio four times per week.

FEMA **TV Talk Show** – Half hour talk show that broadcasts on national television four times a week. Mobile phones are used for feedback and voting.

ChezaSalama **(Play Safe)** – Interactive website with a series of activities and information in English and Swahili—the first of its kind in Tanzania.

Individual Publications – Specialist publications produced on a range of topics: HIV testing, Care 7 Treatment (500,00 copies distributed to all CTC clinics), youth empowerment (*Watata Bomba*, for children/youth with 90,000 copies distributed)

- At the national level, Femina HIP strives to establish themselves as a vocal participant in the public debate in several ways: a) national-scale distribution of their media outlets, particularly the print materials, including circulation to all relevant stakeholders such as NGOs, CBOs and public institutions; b) engagement of politicians in policy dialogue through interviews conducted by the Femina media outlets

Participatory Communication in Femina HIP

The Femina HIP concept is to enhance a participatory governance process via the development of civil society-driven media platforms in print, radio, and television. Four stages of Femina HIP's work in particular illustrate their practice of participatory communication:

Research and implementation: User-driven content production

Common to all the Femina HIP products is a participatory production process, which ensures that young people's voices and concerns are on the sounding board. Femina HIP is very attentive to developing media platforms that reflect the concerns of their readers, thus working carefully on securing spaces where the Femina Clubs and ordinary readers can voice their concerns. Furthermore they work with issues of cultural sensitivity, language sensitivity and generally on producing content based on in-depth and participatory formative research. Rather than simple information dissemination, Femina HIP seeks an ongoing and constant two-way dialogue with its audiences, using the following means:

- The core editorial team conducts systematic visits to listen to the issues of the clubs and the communities. This dialogue feeds directly into the editorial process. The editorial team also reviews letters from the audience, which contribute to developing the themes addressed in the magazines.
- Formative research consists of focus group discussions where they test story lines, texts, interpretation of articles and even vocabulary. The focus group discussions contribute to refining the content. This active participation empowers readers, enhances their understanding of the issues and contributes to their sense of ownership of these projects.
- Both *SiMchezo!* and *FEMA* contain fotonovels produced by local community-based editorial teams of youth.
- Magazines include substantial amounts of material from the readers: experiences told, letters from the clubs, pictures, etc. Several articles are dialogue based and questions from the readers drive the stories the "auntie" and "uncle" write.
- SMS responses are actively encouraged and used in the television talk show.

Youth participation helps to create an environment where issues are taken seriously, where youth take the lead in shaping their own future, and where democratic values are upheld.

Embryonic civil society?

One of Femina HIP's objectives is to build a supportive environment where communities exercise their right to express themselves, participate in public debate and engage in civil society. Historically Tanzania had a weak civil society and few NGOs, and this is gradually changing, opening spaces for an embryonic civil society to develop. Femina works to pursue this change in various ways:

- *FEMA* **Clubs** are established by young people in and out of school as reading and activity groups around the *FEMA* magazine. They read and discuss the issues in the magazine. The groups are sometimes hosted by a school teacher, ensuring the use of *FEMA* magazines in the school setting. Each magazine is read by about 15 readers. Approximately 450 clubs exist, and the aim is to expand to all schools receiving the magazine (2000 +). Some clubs have gone independent and turned into local CBOs in their community. The *FEMA* Club is also the nexus to the national organization, sending representatives to the national events.

- **Outreach activities** include roadshows where staff from the national office travel out to communities and undertake question/answer sessions, providing youth and other community members with the opportunity to voice their concerns, doubts and critiques. People living with HIV/AIDs also participate in these outreach activities, creating a means to speak of the HIV/AIDS pandemic in public. This open approach breaks the silence and enhances dialogue and debate on the topic.

- **Youth empowerment program** consists of a annual youth workshop, an "ambassador program," awards, and school visits.

The combined elements of this community development program establish the crucial link between the lives lived in local communities and the national level of advocacy and public debate in which Femina works.

Participation in the national public debate

Femina's many-faced media platform is a deliberate strategy to achieve visibility and active participation in the public debate. Femina HIP has reached a level of visibility and presence in the mediated public sphere, attracting politicians and leading opinion leaders of Tanzania. Both the prime minister, first lady, many ministers and top civil servants have participated recently in Femina HIP activities: seminars and workshops, as well as interviews in the print magazines.

By maintaining a strong and active constituency of readers and views, Femina HIP has achieved political clout and placed itself centrally in the attempt to hold the government accountable on topics of key concern to the Femina HIP constituency, including HIV/AIDS, sexual and reproductive health, youth education and employment, and other emerging issues such as climate change.

Evaluating participation

Participation's role in evaluating the outcome of Femina HIP is done primarily in an on-going manner, given the constant contact with the constituency and the mechanisms of feedback and input into the editorial processes.

One innovative initiative for Femina HIP is their systematic analysis of letters received from readers of *FEMA* and *SiMchezo!* The focus of the analysis is to assess how the audience of *FEMA* and *SiMchezo!* engage themselves around the issues presented in the magazines. They analyze what degree of audience reflection and action can be found in the letters they write to the magazines. Twelve indicators were identified and a sample of approximately 700 letters was coded. The indicators stem from measuring communication for social change interventions, breaking down participation into a broad range of sub-categories, each measuring an element that contributes to enhancing participatory communication. The indicators included referential reflection, self efficacy, affective parasocial interaction, collective efficacy, visibility, critical thinking, collective action, participation in the public sphere, social connectedness, social cohesion, community dialogue, and leadership.

Aside from the letter analysis, in the evaluation of participation of the Femina HIP project outcomes, numerous issues can be identified. The communication for social change proxy indicators explained in Chapter 2 help us identify, among others, the results of Femina HIP's work:

- Improved *access to information* for a very large number of Tanzania youth and communities
- Change in *social norms*
- Growth in Femina Clubs, in youth involvement around Femina media outlets, in direct participation, as well as in *ownership* of problems aired
- *Collective self-efficacy*, particularly in the communities where the Femina community mobilization team visit but also in the processes that are articulated via national gatherings of the club representatives

Keywords: User-driven content production, participatory formative research, FEMA clubs and outreach: civil society development, voice of and dialogue with readers, clout via participation in the mediated public sphere, assessing audience involvement via letter analysis

Disability, Social Mobilization and Bottom-Up Advocacy

In India, the National Center for Promotion of Employment for Disabled People (NCPEDP) has successfully applied participatory communication strategies to pursue the rights of disabled people. They drew on old Indian traditions of *dharna*, a form of social mobilization that Mahatma Ghandi also used.

NCPEDP is a civil society organization that works to improve livelihoods of disabled people in India. In 2006, NCPEDP decided to seek to influence the five-year Parliamentarian Plan for 2007-2012, which was to outline India's policy related to disabled people. A commission and a series of sub-commissions under the Indian Parliament were to develop the plan. The NCPEDP saw the policy process as a strategic entry point to advocate the rights of disabled people, to promote what they called a "paradigm shift" in Indian disability policy, and to secure improved information, health, financial and employment services for disabled people. The timing in 2006 was strategic, and the advocacy approach developed was participatory, open and inclusive.

NCPEDP's multi-pronged strategy was aimed explicitly at participation in the policy dialogue leading to the formulation of the plan. The primary group to target was the parliamentarians as they controlled participation in the policy dialogue. To apply pressure on the politicians, two activities became central:

- *Networking* with and *mobilization* of all relevant stakeholders involved in improving the livelihoods of disabled people. This networking strategy took place within the National Disability Network (NDN).
- Gain *visibility* in the mediated public sphere. By articulating a public debate and public opinion around the topic, NDPEDP would raise the general awareness among the Indian population as well as put pressure on the decision makers, thus being in many ways a bottom-up advocacy effort.

The networking, mobilization, and visibility were all elements in a coordinated national advocacy campaign initiative. Collective action was sought in the form of campaigning. To meet the challenge, a strong element of capacity building was included, creating a communications unit within NCPEDP. This unit was to disseminate information, uphold the local interest, and support the further organizational development of NDN. NDN was only represented in about half of India's districts at the time.

NCPEDP deliberately sought as broad an ownership as possible of the campaign. One overall national campaign was envisioned. When the initiative took off, however, the National Disability Network's (NDN's) local committees gained strong ownership of the initiative and developed their own local and regional campaigns, expecting technical support from NCPEDP. At the cost of some fatigue in the organization, they achieved large-scale participation in a total of nine campaigns.

Dharna

A central point in the strategy was social mobilization. Based on the old Indian tradition of *dharna*, the NCPEDP sought to engage the surrounding society and the politicians, in particular, to rethink policy. *Dharna* was historically a hunger strike in a public space. The participating protesters would sit and fast in front of the main door of the offender, thereby deliberately attracting public attention. Ghandi made use of this method as a social mobilization tool: it was an early form of participatory communication to advocate for a cause.

Today, *dharna* is not a hunger strike, but still a social mobilization strategy with the aim of attracting public attention. Within the Hindu conceptualization, a demonstration is understood in a more fatalistic manner than in the West. The world has a given (spiritual) order and harmony that can come out of balance. In that context, a *dharna* is the traditional process of purification to restore harmony and balance of the world order. By conducting a *dharna*, the truth is sought.

This philosophy underlies the principles applied by NCPEDP. They built on old religious and cultural traditions, adapting these to present times with modern means of communication and policy dialogue, revealing the power and potential of their communication strategy.

Events illustrated the genius of their strategy. The day after the large nationally organized *dharna* in front of parliament, relevant parliamentarians called NCPEDP. They made no reference to the *dharna* of the previous day but simply invited NCPEDP to participate in the policy development process, which ultimately led to the Plan 2007-2012.

NCPEDP went through a rather vigorous and laborious process, much of which was advocacy based, to submit recommendations for the five-year plan. This process resulted not only in their recommendations being included but also in a chapter on disability being included. This was a significant achievement as it was the first time in the history of India's Five Year Plans that disability was included with a separate, dedicated chapter.

Participatory Communication in NCPEDP's Work

The level and forms of NCPEDP's participatory communication strategy can be assessed in various ways. In terms of concrete political initiatives, there are the following outcomes:

- Achievement of the overall goal to actively participate in the national policy dialogue to formulate the 11th Plan regarding Indian policy toward disabled people.
- Seven out of nine *dharnas* in the course of a two-year period have led to changes in policies or the formulation of new policies for people with disabilities.
- Eleven Indian states now have disability commissions, which are responsible for policy at state level.

Assessing the results of NCPEDP based on their intangible goals of empowerment and social change, the proxy-indicators from Chapter two help us to outline the following results:

- Increased sense of *ownership* among relevant organizations and individuals involved in the fight for improved conditions for people with disabilities
- Increased *leadership* of the disability organizations and their constituencies in the attempt to change policies and achieve rights
- Some change of *social norms* seems to have occurred via visibility in the media and widespread public debate
- *Participation* in the national network dialogue
- Participation in the national or the regional (state-level) with *dharnas* as a physical presence in the streets

Keywords: Seeking dialogue with parliamentarians; broad-based participatory strategy, including networking with and mobilization of relevant stakeholders; visibility in the mediated public sphere; massive local ownership.

Lessons Learned

As the cases illustrate, participatory communication strategies can contribute to a synergetic development process where a series of interconnected goals are pursued. Thus, the cases show a combination of opportunities provided by participatory communication:

- As illustrated in all three cases, in the pursuit of provision of basic services, participatory communication helps to sustain the process of claiming those services.
- Participatory communication helps generate policy relevant-information via the participation of ordinary citizens in social mobilization, public debate and policy dialogue. The articulation of voice from ordinary citizens feeds into policy formulation processes as bottom-up advocacy processes—not least in the Indian case but also to some degree in the Tanzanian case.
- Participatory communication becomes a tool to monitor progress toward goals, for example, in the active community response to the media outlets of Femina HIP.
- A highlight of participatory communication is that it facilitates reflection and learning among local groups, providing opportunities for dialogue, learning and critique, which again becomes central elements of evaluating a project or program.

Cutting across these generic qualities inherent in participatory communication, five core lessons can be learned from the cases presented:

Participatory communication: Both a means and an end

Distinguishing participatory communication as a means from participatory communication as an end *per se* connects to the distinction of short-term project objectives versus long-term organizational objectives. The short-term project cycle of maybe two, three or four years will often focus on using participatory communication as *a means to achieve results.* The long-term objectives of an organization will often strive for sustained participation of key stakeholders where participatory communication becomes *an end in itself.* It becomes a process that sustains the long-term goals of the organization.

To achieve a sustained outcome, the short-term project focus has to be coherent with the long-term process of empowerment. The shorter term adopts tactical activities that have to be reconciled with in longer term with goals and processes of empowerment.

In communication terms, the long-term participatory communication processes are often more difficult to achieve and sustain than the singular or specific participatory communication activities. The long-term participatory communication processes require on-going commitments of the participating people (staff of the responsible organization or participants of their projects). They also speak to structural changes and to securing the voice and participation of the relevant communities. In assessing the cases both the long-term and short-term perspectives are considered, as is the nature and characteristics of the participatory communication we can identify.

Integration of improved service delivery with advocating for a cause

The conceptual distinction between participation as a tool versus participation as a goal *per se* speaks to another often encountered dilemma of development work. It is the dilemma between pursuing successful deliveries of specific sector initiatives such as information, health, or agricultural services versus the more process-oriented social mobilization and advocacy for a cause. It is a subtle distinction, but an increasing number of civil society organizations are now experiencing the need to move from a more narrowly defined focus on service delivery to a broader-based advocacy agenda, pursuing policy changes, accountability, and transparency to secure deeper social and structural changes. Often they combine both agendas.

Many smaller organizations are traditionally involved in service delivery, particularly in communities and countries with weak public service structures. However, rather than continuously fulfilling the delivery of services that the public sector ought to be delivering, civil society organizations are increasingly developing advocacy strategies, which in turn pursue the structural change that permits good governance and public provision of services. This process requires a multi-pronged strategy of social mobilization, collective action and increased involvement in public debate, as well as other means such as advocacy from below, to achieve the attention of opinion leaders, decision makers and the general public.

The question to consider here is how participatory communication strategies work in reconciling requirements for service delivery with the advocacy goals for social change. Although stated above as a dilemma, the real challenge may well be to provide service delivery while at the same time advocating for social and structural change in a way that the service delivery ultimately becomes a responsibility undertaken by the government.

Multi-level change processes

In a participatory communication intervention, it is often assumed that the key focus is the community. This is often correct, but there are also many cases where an initiative of an NGO or a public office engages stakeholders at the regional or national levels. Therefore, it can be useful to distinguish participatory communication at three different levels:

- Level of the individual and his or her family;
- Community level, be it a neighborhood, village, municipality or district;
- National level.

NCPEDP's experience in India illustrated the multiple levels of intervention well. Theirs was an ambitious attempt to mobilize a national movement for increased rights for the disabled. Different from NCPEDP's national level work, Minga Peru focuses exclusively on a region in the Peruvian Amazon. Minga Peru has worked steadily and continuously in the same region over a decade-long period. Femina HIP balances between wanting to mobilize nationally in order to hold the government accountable, and at the same time, to support a local civil society development processes in just three of Tanzania's provinces.

Furthermore, one activity in a project, which may be more participatory, may well take place in synergy with other activities of the project. Some assessment of this synergy among the different subcomponents is important. Too often the individual objectives in a project are implemented and evaluated in isolation from the other objectives in the same project, despite clear connections.

Management, leadership and organization in participatory communication processes

Leadership, management and organizational capacity are skills that are required—but underestimated—in participatory communication processes. Frequently an organization serves as the catalyst of a participatory process, and to achieve positive outcomes, it must grow. Unfortunately the needs for management skills, organizational development and capacity building may be recognized at late stages. NCPEDP was overwhelmed by the way NDN's local committees took ownership of the campaigns and required technical support in amounts NCPEDP could barely meet.

Civil society development takes time

The process of Minga Peru was very participatory from the outset, but the local community took its time in seeing the value of engaging in the process. In Tanzania, Femina HIP supports the development of civil society, but the process, underway now for a decade, is very gradual. Both of these cases began more than a decade ago, confirming how participatory communication processes may take time and have to evolve—albeit often facilitated—according to the trust, commitment, ownership and capacity of the engaged communities.

Keywords: Participation as a means, participation as an end; tangible results; intangible results; service delivery, advocacy levels of intervention: individual/family, community, and national

References

Anyaegbunam, C., Mefalopulos, P. and Moetsabi T. (2004, 2nd ed.). *Participatory Rural Communication Appraisal: Starting with the people.* Harare, Zimbabwe: FAO/SADC.

Beltrán, L. R. (1979). "A Farewell to Aristotle: Horizontal Communication." Published originally in UNESCO Working Papers No. 48, International Commission for the Study of Communication Problems. Reprinted in: A., Gumucio-Dagron, Alfonso and T. Tufte (2006, eds.). *Communication for Social Change Anthology: Historical and Contemporary Readings.* New Jersey: Communication for Social Change Consortium.

Boal, A. (1974). *Teatro del Oprimido – Teoria y práctica.* Buenos Aires. Ediciones de la Flor.

Chambers, R. (1983). *Rural Development: Putting the Last First.* Essex, England: Longman House.

Cooke, B. and Kothari, U. (2001, eds.). *Participation. The New Tyranny?* London: Zed Books.

Escobar, A. (1995). *Encountering Development. The Making and Unmaking of the Third World.* New Jersey: Princeton University Press.

Figueroa, M.E., Kincaid, L., Rani, M. and Lewis, G. (2002). *Communication for Social Change: An Integrated Model for Measuring the Process and Its Outcomes.* New York: Rockefeller Foundation.

Freire P. (1973). "Extension o comunicacion?" Originally published by the Institute for Agricultural Reform (Santiago), 1969. Translation by Louise Bigwood and Margaret Marshall (2003) published as "Extension or Communication" in *Education for Critical Consciousness,* Seabury.

Freire, P. (1997). *Pedagogy of the Oppressed* (Rev. ed.). New York, NY: Continuum.

Gumucio-Dagron A. and T. Tufte (2006, eds.). *Communication for Social Change Anthology. Historical and Contemporary Readings.* New Jersey: Communication for Social Change Consortium

Hendricks, P. (1998). "Developing Youth Curriculum Using the Targeting Life Skills Model." http://www.extension.iastate.edu/4H/skls.eval.htm.

Lasswell, H. (1948). "The Structure and Function of Communication in Society." In L. Bryson (Ed.), *The Communication of Ideas* (pp. 37–51). New York, NY: Harper.

Mazzei, L. and Scuppa, G. (2006). "The Role of Communication in Large Intrastructure. The Bumbuna Hydroelectric Project in Post-Conflict Sierra Leone." World Bank Working Paper No. 84. The World Bank.

Mefalopulos, P. (2008). *Development Communication Sourcebook: Broadening the Boundaries of Communications.* Washington DC: The World Bank.

Mody, B. (1991). *Designing Messages for Development Communication.* New Delhi, India: Sage Publications.

Narayan, D. (2005, ed.). *Measuring Empowerment. Cross-Disciplinary Perspectives.* Oxford: The World Bank & Oxford University Press.

Rodriguez, C. (2001). *Fissures in the Mediascape. An International Study of Citizens' Media.* Hampton Press, Creskill, NJ, USA.

Rogers, E. (1962). *The Diffusion of Innovations.* Glencoe, IL: Free Press.

Sengupta, A. (2007). "Enacting an Alternative Vision of Communication for Social Change in the Peruvian Amazon." Doctoral Dissertation. Ohio University. http://www.ohiolink.edu/etd/view.cgi?acc_num=ohiou1178730094

Ugboajah, F. O. (1985). "Oramedia in Africa." In F.O. Ugboajah, ed., *Mass Communication, Culture and Society in West Africa.* London: WACC. Reprinted in A. Gumucio-Dagron and T. Tufte (2006), eds., *Communication for Social Change Anthology: Historical and Contemporary Readings.* New Jersey: Communication for Social Change Consortium.

Webpages
www.cfsc.org – The Communication for Social Change Consortium.

www.chezasalama.com – FEMINA Health Information Project's homepage.

www.mingaperu.org – Minga Peru's homepage.

Eco-Audit

Environmental Benefits Statement

The World Bank is committed to preserving Endangered Forests and natural resources. We print World Bank Working Papers and Country Studies on postconsumer recycled paper, processed chlorine free. The World Bank has formally agreed to follow the recommended standards for paper usage set by Green Press Initiative—a nonprofit program supporting publishers in using fiber that is not sourced from Endangered Forests. For more information, visit www.greenpressinitiative.org.

In 2008, the printing of these books on recycled paper saved the following:

Trees*	Solid Waste	Water	Net Greenhouse Gases	Total Energy
355	16,663	129,550	31,256	247 mil.
*40 feet in height and 6–8 inches in diameter	Pounds	Gallons	Pounds CO$_2$ Equivalent	BTUs

green press
INITIATIVE